Until It Wasn't

A Memoir

For Wes, who taught me profound lessons about life and love in our thirty years together. For Kara, Sean, and Jake who embody all the best parts of their dad.

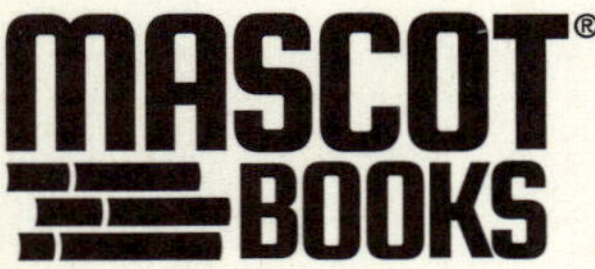

www.mascotbooks.com

Until It Wasn't

I have tried to recreate events, locales, and conversations from my memories of them. In order to maintain their anonymity in some instances I have changed the names of individuals and places, I may have changed some identifying characteristics and details such as physical properties, occupations, and places of residence.

For more information, please contact:
Mascot Books
560 Herndon Parkway #120
Herndon, VA 20170
info@mascotbooks.com

Library of Congress Control Number: 2016919222

CPSIA Code: PRBANG0217A
ISBN-13: 978-1-68401-101-8

Printed in the United States

Until It Wasn't

love, loss, and finding hope again

Sharon Neff

One

I was in my son's room, and on the floor by his closet was a "bud." I was pissed, of course, and really, really over the pot thing. But instead of tossing it, I thought that maybe I might need it for Wes. My decision to not flush it down the toilet or confront Jake on the issue again turned out to have a lasting and memorable effect on our current situation. Friends had given Wes a joint early on in his illness and when I found out about it, I hit the roof. I didn't want this to be about the pot and everyone pushing it on him, because it seemed like the edgy thing to do. Honestly, I heard more about this subject from the most random people and I got a little sick of it. But, for some reason, I decided to shove the bud in my pocket.

Well, I knew that Sean had rolling papers down in his room, mainly because I had had a couple of conversations with him about it. Gotta love a kid who is pretty open with his parents and will talk with you about it. The truth is, when it comes to pot – I'm really not very cool. That ship had sailed a very long time ago. But Sean had quit as well, and that is really why we were able to have a reasonable conversation about it. The conversation went something like this:

"Sean, what are these?"

"You know what they are Mom, they're rolling papers."

"Hmmmm, why do you have them?"

"I've had them for a long time and you know that because you've seen them and gone through my room."

"Hmmmm, true story."

It started as diverticulitis. Five months of trying to cure the diverticulitis and figure out why his whole abdominal area was so sore. Three CT scans, one colonoscopy, one endoscopy, one trip to the emergency room, countless trips back and forth to the doctors, and no one saw the mass growing and showing up on the scans, until the last CT on October 26th, 2009. Someone, finally paid attention to the details.

We get a call from Wes' doctor to tell him that this routine CT scan showed a mass. I had answered the phone, and the doctor asked for Wes. I took it up to him, and I stood there and watched him as he listened on the phone. We were in our bedroom and Wes was standing by our bathroom door as he listened to the words that would change the course of his life forever. I remember him dropping his head and shaking it back and forth before hanging up the phone. I said, "What?" And he told me. They had found a mass. He had no other information because he had stopped listening after that. I called the doctor right back to get more details, even though I wasn't listening so well either.

Wes had a duodenal mass that was complicated by being wrapped by the mesentery artery. I thought of a golf ball being wrapped around by my hand and fingers. I have never lost that image, ever, as it has taken up permanent residence in my head.

It is amazing how in one minute, your life can be changed forever. There you have it: it was for us. Forever changed. Never to go back.

Cancer dictates your life in ways you can never anticipate. Raw emotions plagued us on every level, never able to find a comfortable place to house themselves, as they seemed to always be on my shoulders, my stomach, and in my head.

The visceral image of Wes taking that call, and absorbing the words he was hearing, is forever etched in my mind. All of my protective instincts came out from places I didn't know they were stored, and went into overdrive. I have to shield him from this bad news, I have to absorb it all so that he doesn't have to, and I have to be strong; for him, for the kids and for myself. Strangely, that overprotective instinct never left and never wavered, but only intensified. I was in his corner, and in his camp.

Over the course of the next couple of weeks, we had countless appointments with doctors and specialists, and had more scans and more info to absorb. We met with the doctor that was going to be Wes' oncologist. He was stark, he was frank, and didn't mince words…just the way I hate it. Mince the fucking words already, I don't want to hear this bad news. But no one listened, especially the doctor.

Wes always wanted to know the bottom line. He never minced words either. I remember sitting in the doctor's office, it was a 4:00 appointment and it was getting dark outside. The doctor's office seemed to only have one light in it, on his desk. It seemed dark and foreboding, just like the news we were receiving. I remember hating the office and not liking the doctor so much either. I've never liked the bearers of bad news and this guy never even had a chance.

Wes asked right then and there what his chances were. His doctor said it could be twenty to forty percent. I watched Wes' reaction to this news, as I couldn't absorb any more myself, but I knew I had to help him absorb this. He actually may have handled it better than me. Imagine driving home from that appointment, with your person, and you have no words to comfort him because you've just been gut punched and you are still trying to get air.

Wes had a huge group of friends from childhood, and they are affectionately called "the Goons," or accurately called: you decide. They were all called in to meet back at our house, because I felt we needed all the Goon love for Wes to get in a fighting mode, because this beast was going to need Mike Tyson to beat it. All the Goons surrounded us and gave us love, encouragement, and support to hit this head on. It helped me, but I'm not sure if Wes wanted to handle that night alone, or not, but I guess I didn't give him the choice.

I got a call that same night from the director of Life with Cancer. He told me not to listen to statistics, and that statistics start with you, and people beat statistics all the time. Profound. I was thankful for those uplifting words. I have repeated them to myself over and over, and have passed that wisdom on to many other people that face this horrible disease. He was a social worker by training and was always a calming voice for us during this process. He mapped out what we would face, corroborating what the doctor had told us and helping us navigate all the info that we had been given. That's the beauty of Life with Cancer: it is the thread that gets you from one place to the next throughout the cancer journey. They are the navigators for you, they are your strength, and they become your hope.

It helps to hear the phases or stages one will go through. Fear is definitely out there. My biggest source of fear has always been when the doctors present one with this news and then there's the absence of hope. That screams louder to me than the word cancer.

It is now November and I have notes all around the

house that have the word "chemo" on them. How did we get to this? Just a few weeks ago we were discussing Thanksgiving plans or trading in cars, all the mundane stuff that I long for once again. Now this is permeating our conversations in writing and out loud. It is a drastic change in the day to day.

It has been a rough few weeks, but we are feeling stronger now. Everyone says this is the low point in the cancer ordeal; before you have a plan of action and can start to feel somewhat in control of your life again. We head up to John's Hopkins to meet with the specialist. We are hopeful the chemo will shrink the tumor. Away would be great, but at least enough to get it off of the arteries it is involving, then surgery in a few months. That is the rough game plan. Hopkins was fantastic. They didn't tell us they were going to cure us, but they sure made us feel like they could. That was huge.

It is the end of November and Wes had his first chemo session today. He did great. It is a grim place to be, to be sure. My mother used to always say, if you are ever feeling sorry for yourself, go sit in the waiting room of a hospital. Or a chemo office, I add. Actually, it is called the Infusion Center. Man, do I care; you can't butter up that name, no matter how much you try.

The nurses were great and very positive in the infusion center. A big change from the doctor's offices they work for. I don't get why these oncologists are so negative. It's not right to put people through that. Wes and I knew what we were up against, but we would rather stay positive than think these horrid thoughts. And let me tell you, these are some dark places, thinking cancer thoughts. Positivity is the key.

Wes needed to get moving forward with the chemo to make him feel like he was moving forward with a remedy. Sitting around just waiting is brutal. I mean really, what are you waiting for, the tumor to grow? Let's get a move on and kick the cancer's ass.

I am sending out a prayer wish list to God, which is for the chemo to shrink the tumor. I've decided that I will only ask God to grant our wishes in increments – maybe He will be more inclined to bestow His blessing on us, if I don't ask for the whole pie all at once. What do You say God, are You listening?

I say prayers all day long on a good day and in noncritical times. I eat, drink and sleep my prayers now. I read a book on faith and cancer and it said that God wants us well and that the devil is the one fighting us. Don't let him win; stay positive. That is definitely the goal.

I sleep with two scapulars and my rosary. I find them in the bed, or actually Wes finds them in the bed. I didn't even think he realized what it was the first time, but he told me where it was one night when I was looking for it. He was sweet. He at first thought it was my "jewelry purse," but must have looked inside to see what it was. I will sleep with all my accoutrements every night until he is well.

It is Christmas time and I am trying to get all things holiday in order, get Wes to his appointments, work, and be there for the kids. The Christmas tree has been standing in the corner of the living room with no lights on it for two days just screaming at me for attention, like I don't have enough things screaming at me. You should hear all the voices in my head.

I need to get the tree decorated and move to the next thing, starting with cleaning the house of all the containers holding Christmas decorations and removing the clutter. Somehow that clutter seems to amplify the stress I feel inside and I have an unyielding need to straighten and get order. It would stand to reason that the clutter represents all that is wrong in my life right then and there.

I finished my bathroom project downstairs: tiling, grouting, caulking and painting and now trying to hang stuff like mirrors and hand towel holders. It looks pretty good, but the work seems like an out of body experience. It's funny how you can do these mundane tasks in light of the tragedy that is going on around you.

I really feel like this is going to be okay. Every emotion is piqued though. Every protective bone in my body is heightened, not just for Wes but for the kids and strangely enough, even for myself. I want to self-protect also. I struggle to watch Wes feel badly and feel low. The psyche stuff is the worst for me. It hurts me so much to see Wes feel like he is ruining the family. I see fear in his eyes.

I've been getting Christmas cards in the mail and I

just don't have it in me to send them out this year. I am stretched to the limit and I just can't think about sending out a card. I will need to send one to Daddy, because he gets upset about the Christmas card thing. I don't want to get him upset, he is my rock and Wes' illness has really upended him. He loves Wes and keeps calling to check in on him and he tells me he is saying tons of prayers. I know he is, he even kneels down at his bedside for his prayers. I am hoping kneeling down by your bed gives you more prayer power. It is my hope anyway and I hope God is listening.

I can tell Wes is getting better at telling people about his illness. I have always loved and admired how he connects to people. He is so genuine and true that people just respond to him. Watching him tell people breaks my heart, but also makes me beam, I am so proud of him. He is the single most awesome person I know and the one person I have truly wanted to emulate. How lucky am I for that?

Christmas and Christmas Eve are fast approaching and we are having people over. I want there to be craziness in the house so that I can forget about the tough stuff. This cancer is tough, and I'm not sure how people do it. Did I mention that I didn't feel like I was doing a very good job at it?

Christmas day ended up being a great day. It started out sad and I was trying to hold back the tears as I was up before everyone, getting all the Christmas lights on, the Christmas carols on the stereo, coffee going and breakfast on the table. But as I stood in the kitchen alone, I got hit with a rush of random, or maybe not so random, emotions thinking about how we used to have such a happy home that now was just sad. That realization made my cry, but also made me mad, and I decided I needed to make this what it is. We need to be thankful for small things like an hour or a day or whatever, and so I changed gears to embrace the day.

Wes and I were not going to exchange gifts that year but there were truly things that he needed, like new pillows, new slippers, jeans that fit and sweaters that were now a size large instead of extra-large. More changes, and clearly changes in the physical.

We are never sure what Jake is taking in and assimilating on an emotional level. He does not show his emotions to many and keeps them pretty close to his chest. So with Wes' illness, we weren't sure the extent to which he was embracing our new situation. But when Wes opened up Jake's gift to him, it was a black, hooded "Live Strong" sweatshirt and Wes held it up for the camera, in front of his face, to hide the tears that were now clouding his eyes.

Two

Wes started radiation, and the first week wasn't too bad. Once again, I could barely stand to be in those waiting rooms. So dank, so dark, and so grim. Wes would talk with other patients, and I could barely even muster a nod of the head. It was so depressing. All of these places just screamed of the loss of hope that I'd seen in so many millions of pictures of the holocaust. The absence of hope, staring us right in the face again. I can't get away from it, it is always staring us squarely in the eye, and I can't run away fast enough. It is so hard to balance these competing emotions of despair and find the ability to accost this beast to eradicate it, and stay focused, determined, and never giving up. In other words, being hopeful. It's hard to sustain that hope in a chemo or radiation office. Just take my word for it.

Wes' schedule consisted of going to Fairfax Hospital every day and getting radiation, then heading three miles down the road to his doctor's office to get chemo. Can you imagine? He had radiation and chemo every day, five days a week, for five weeks. The truth is, it almost killed him.

As we progressed through this rigorous treatment, Wes got so sick that he could barely eat anything. He could barely summon the energy to get into the car, but he did. He was so tough, it was a testimony to his drive. He ended up not being able to eat anything. In one week, he had one bowl of cereal and one milkshake. I was so beside myself. I didn't know what to do. I talked with Wes' older sister Marcia one day and said, "I can't do it, I can't get him to eat, he won't listen to me." She offered to come over and help, and sure enough, when Marcia said, "Wesley, you have to eat, please try to eat." He got up and started trying to eat. Good Lord. But I was actually just relieved to have him eat something, even though he could not keep anything down. It wasn't even a case of him keeping it down, it was a case of him even having the ability to even try. He slept twenty-three hours a day during this time, and was only up for the time we took him to radiation and chemo.

Something had to give. Our nurse Mary called our doctor and said "uncle" for us.

We admitted Wes to the hospital that Friday. Jake and Sean helped me get him to the doctor's office and we admitted him from there. That morning, before taking him to the doctor's office, Wes was sitting on the side of our bed and he looked at me and said, "Sharon, I can't do this anymore." He was resigned and exhausted. I said, "You don't have to, we are going to get you to the hospital and take care of you."

When we got to the hospital, we had to go to admissions. Wes was so weak and had to sit on a chair, waiting for me to finish with the administrative nonsense. It seemed like such a surreal experience sitting there, doing those seemingly silly tasks when inside my world, everything was imploding. But we did them. As if life doesn't present you with enough ironies, it wasn't going to let this experience go without one either. As we finished up the paper work, the administrator called for a volunteer to come with a wheelchair and take Wes up to his room. I said a few times, "It's okay, I can take him up in the wheelchair," but they were having none of it. The volunteer showed up and looked a hundred years old and her head didn't even go over the back of Wes' head while he was sitting down. She had white hair and was almost as frail as him, but clearly for different reasons. I looked at Wes and we caught each other's eye and we both started laughing. Wes never missed a beat and ironic moments were always something we both zeroed in on and would laugh about. So, as it would play out, in my head, I am envisioning this being a Tim Conway moment in a Carol Burnett skit and I kid you not, this chick couldn't even get the traction to get his wheelchair moving. Wes just dropped his head and shook it a little, with a big smile on his face. Ironies in life, they have a tendency to reveal themselves to you while you are in your own tragedy. I guess we were thankful for those moments, no matter what or when we could grab them. We actually did make it up to Wes' room but it was not expedient travelling.

Wes was in the hospital for a week. He tells us that he didn't think he was going to make it, that he was certain he was dying. That's what it felt like anyway. But he responded quickly and well from the remedies they gave him in the hospital. The first few days were tough, but they gave him "food in a bag." IV's with tons of calories and vitamins and everything you need to regain strength. The kicker for me is that sugar is the cancer's fuel source, so the commonsensical approach would be to starve the cancer of sugar. It would stand to reason, at least in my mind. But that is not what hospitals do, and they promote the ingesting of as many calories as you can get in you as a cancer patient in order to keep your weight up. It was all so counterintuitive to me and I wanted to scream all the time. Are you kidding me?! This is textbook, don't feed the cancer sugar. But they do and they pushed and that was ultimately what was inside of Wesley's food in a bag. I was at wits end. Things were spiraling out of control and I couldn't stop the spinning. I felt like a spectator in a lot of ways during those weeks, watching everything go down. I like to take a commonsensical approach to life and put things back in order. The problem is, there is no order to cancer. No order to the chaos it brings. No order to the demise. It happens right under your nose while you are watching it all happen and then one day you say, "How the hell did everything get so out of control?"

No control. Imagine what that really means. What in your life do you not have some control over? Probably not much. This came on so fast and with such intensity that I was hardly even prepared to confront it, address it, or even introduce myself to it. It became intimate with us quickly and with hardly a proper introduction. I remember thinking that things had to get better somehow. I was prepared for it to be bad, but I was never prepared for it to be that bad. No words do it justice. I just kept watching my husband wither in a matter of weeks and days. I was giving him ice chips just to get something in him. I felt alone, scared and incredibly inept. No question. How could I be letting this happen? Why can't I make it better? I am failing and worst of all I am failing Wes. Please God, don't let me fail Wes. I owe him so much, please let me find the thing that makes him better. God, if you take him now, I won't have had the chance to make it better. Please God, don't let me fail Wes. Please God, don't let me fail Wes.

It's true that no amount of Gorilla Glue is going to help you put things back in order from cancer. It is a whirlwind and it is destructive and insidious. This isn't for the faint of heart. Not that I am a strong person, because I am not, but my strength always came from Wes. He has always loved me enough to make me feel strong. I guess that is the secret to love, at least in my case anyway. Wes loving me gave me confidence that I otherwise may not have had or found. He's just got to get better. I need him.

Three

Wes got home from the hospital the Friday before Easter. Kara was home for the weekend and went with me to pick him up. My sister Patty came over to help get things ready for us to have Easter at our house. We wanted Wes to be comfortable and if he needed to go up to rest, he would be at home. Wes had to eat real food at the hospital and be able to keep it down before they would release him to come home. He did, and that brings us to the Saturday breakfast. I made scrambled eggs and toast and we thought Wes was doing okay with it all, but then he got up and ran to the bathroom to be sick. I was really rattled and upset. Did I really think that it was going to go smoothly once he got home? Of course I did.

So as I am trying not to cry, I remembered that I was armed with a bud of pot and a rolling paper, compliments of both of our sons. More irony. I'm thankful for the little things in life. So I went down to the basement to try my hand at rolling this joint. I never got the hang of the rolling thing thirty years ago, and I really didn't think my rolling prowess had changed much over the last thirty years of not smoking pot, but there I was, in my house with stuff that I had scarfed up from my kids. My life was not turning out the way I had imagined. Trust me on this.

I got the thing rolled. But since there wasn't much pot to begin with, I ended up with two very long ends that were rolled very tightly. I twisted and twisted and twisted. I was pretty sure that was how it was supposed to be done.

Wes was outside on the patio on the lounge chair when I brought my newly rolled creation out to him. Now get this, it is 11:00 a.m., in the middle of suburbia, and I hand Wes the joint and try to light it for him while he is holding it up to his mouth. I have my sister Patty there, who has gotten into all sorts of trouble in her life because of pot, and she thinks this whole scene is hysterical. Kara is watching this spectacle and is in awe. All would have gone smoothly, except for the fact that Wes was inhaling so hard to get some air through the very, very long rolled ends that he almost passed out. His face turned red, his eyes got big and he got nothing. Except a headache.

In the end, Wes did get a little bit out of that joint and he was able to eat, which was a godsend. I never would have believed it, but I have witnessed it first hand, numerous times, and as much as I hate it, the pot always took away Wes' nausea, his pain and made him hungry, without much of an effort either. I actually welcomed it.

That day, we discussed the need to get more pot, and of course we all looked at Kara. She said, "Huh, why me?" We said it was because we didn't really want the boys to know. So she proceeded to text some friends. Her crew were never really into this stuff, which made this even more ironic. She was in the dining room studying for exams and she kept yelling, "Mom, I really think you should be getting the boys to do this, I don't really know how to do this!" I kept saying, "Can't do that Kara, Sean is steering clear of this stuff and we are trying to keep Jake from doing this, so just keep looking." Of course, it was from Jake's floor that I absconded with the pot bud. Thank you son. I mean really, who does this? In the end, Kara wasn't comfortable with this and we ended up getting it elsewhere. Kara would do anything for Wes, but this proved to be more than she bargained for. When it appeared, I asked no questions. It is almost unimaginable how you can be diametrically opposed to something and yet be so eternally grateful for it as well. I was grateful for the reprieve pot afforded Wes. Grateful beyond belief. Really? Cancer has turned my life upside down.

The pot was a blessing and Wes was able to eat and he gained weight and strength. He was able to go on the annual Goon Open golf tournament, with all of his friends at the beach and he played all four days and had a great time. All the Goons took great care of him, especially Mark who stayed at our house with him and ministered all meds and supplements. As happy as I was to see Wes go, to be doing something fun and which represented normalcy to us, it was so hard to let him go. Still worrying, still overprotecting.

As it turned out, we got more pot. Now we have a stash and Wes uses it when it's needed. He doesn't really like it and I often have to push him to do some in order to get him to eat. I feel like I am in some bizarre movie. I would never have believed it possible, but desperate times call for desperate measures. Or something like that.

After that upswing in Wes' strength and weight gain, things started unraveling at a more consistent pace. We seemed to always be trying to play catch up. But catch up to what, I'm not exactly sure, as we were never to see an upswing again, on anything really. The chemo was going poorly. Wes was getting weaker and he was seriously ready to give up the chemo and live out the rest of his time, for however long that might be. I did not have these in-depth conversations with Wes on this subject, because I was not in the give-up, or give-in mode. But any time I thought Wes was going in that direction, I'd ride him about it. "Wesley, do not give up, we are figuring this thing out, and you've got to keep fighting." He always assured me that he was, but several times he would say to me, "Sharon, I love how hard you are fighting for me, but I think this is worse than you think." I would shoot back that we were trying different things and always researching and we were going to find the right combo. As I made my many proclamations of success in beating the cancer, Wes always got a look on his face that said, as much as he loved me for it, it worried him that I was not dealing in the reality of his cancer. I was never going to give up. Ever.

I often think about those times and I get very sad, especially since it is quite possible that I didn't give Wes the outlet he needed to voice his concerns and maybe tell me the things he needed to. Although we had had all of our affairs in order long before cancer, I suspect there were things he wanted to say, but maybe didn't have the fight in him, to fight cancer, pain, nausea, weakness and a wife that had tunnel vision. I just couldn't wrap my head around succumbing to the possibility of this not working out. Of Wes not getting better. Of Wes not being here one day. How could I? Wes was my life. He was all the goodness in life. He encompassed that and I was, for some unbelievable reason, lucky enough to be his partner. No, I was never going to give up on the cancer fight and I was never going to give up on Wes. I always believed in Wesley, and I truly, truly believed that he would come out on top. Why wouldn't I? Wes never let me down.

So Wes would talk to the Goons and maybe they appreciated that their best buddy had a wife that was like a junk yard dog and was going to hit anyone that brought any negative energy to the hospital or to our home. Maybe they just thought I was crazy. I was, no doubt, but I was going to keep fighting. I remember so many times when the doctors would pull me outside and look me straight in the eye and say, "Mrs. Neff, you do understand, don't you? Your husband may only have a couple of weeks or a month to live. You do understand that Mrs. Neff?" I'd say, "Fuck you," to myself, but I'm pretty sure they could see it on my face. My standard answer was always, and usually packed with enough ammo behind it that no one got the wrong impression, "Well, he's still living isn't he, and as long as he's still living, we're going to keep fighting for him." Truly, they thought I was wacked. I came upon that look on many a doctor's face and honestly, they are lucky I didn't throw a punch. I was never going to let Wesley ever see me give up on him. I truly don't know if I could think of a bigger betrayal of love and loyalty, than to give up. I could not face what was happening on so many levels, that is all true, but I think subconsciously some acceptance and understanding and some internal preparedness was going on. That, even though I wanted to shut it down and not acknowledge the truth, it was trying desperately to creep into my psyche and force me to deal in the reality. I kept thinking, why are all these people trying to tell me all this bad news? Get off it already. But there was a small part of me that was starting to pay attention to these messages. I just hated anyone that was trying to tell me Wes wasn't going to make it. Don't you dare talk about my husband like that and don't you dare intimate that he isn't going to make it. Don't talk behind his back in whispers and hushed tones and act like he is not a living, breathing, viable person. I couldn't get my cocoon spun largely and quickly enough to protect him from all of this. And maybe for myself as well. I suspected people were saying things about him, behind his back. "Oh, he's not going to make it," or, "Oh, she isn't dealing with it or the reality." My protective mode ramped up exponentially at this time. But maybe it was true, as Wes died, at home, on February 2, 2011.

As I finally came to some conclusions about Wes and his cancer battle, I also still held out hope. In the end, Wes was in the hospital for three weeks, and although we did get a new doctor that actually loved Wes immediately and was willing to try for a possible, positive outcome. He did tell Wes that he didn't want to fill him with false hope but he did think there were still a couple of things we could try. Wes was willing, sort of. I think, maybe, he did it for me, for us, for the kids, but I suspect he knew what his body was telling him. The duodenal cancer had spread to his liver, and his bones, as we came to find out in the last six weeks. We knew it had spread to his liver, but the bones hit us hard. We had no idea. So, we started Wes on a chemo treatment at the hospital and he completed only one. He had a roomful of Goons as he started the procedure and they were all there giving him moral support. We had both of our families and friends at the hospital, it was a constant revolving door, but welcoming for me. Wes had had an intestinal blockage when he was admitted and it took quite a concerted effort to try to get it removed. One night, Kara wanted to take me to a movie, and although it seemed out of balance with what was going on around us, I went. When we got out of the theatre I called Sean, who was still at the hospital, to see how it was going. He and Wes' sister Emily were still at the hospital at 9:30 at night and Sean said Dad had been getting sick all evening. He seemed worn out emotionally, and I told him I'd be right up. I dropped

Kara off at the house, and packed a bag and headed up, driving that now familiar route to Fairfax Hospital. When I got there, they both, and actually Wes also, looked exhausted. When both Emily and Sean left, I helped Wes get comfortable, and I got settled into the recliner that took up permanent residence in his room. While I was sitting there, Wes said, "Sharon, come lay with me." I said, "Really? You want me to get in the bed with you?" He said that he did, and so I tried to be as unobtrusive as I could and not put pressure on any part of his body that would cause him pain. We laid there together for a while, playing make believe and trying to act like we were in our bed, in our home, in our bedroom, and that all was well in our world. But the machines and tubes and noises and discomfort made it impossible. I was so thankful to be laying there next to him, breathing his air and feeling his body next to mine, and trying to imagine a happier time. I was thankful for the invitation and was thankful to feel his arms around me holding me as tight as he could muster, but still in the strong grasp that was so familiar to me, and what I still yearned for. My being in the bed was hurting him, so I got out, with sadness, and went to the recliner in the corner. At the crack of dawn Mark walked in, surprised to see me, but we discussed what had come to be the night before and we knew, and even I did, that things were not looking good. Wes and Mark already knew that. But Mark never let on, except when he thought I needed to deal in reality, or at least some semblance of it. I am thankful for Mark. He allowed me to be delusional and never made me feel guilty about it.

As all things progressed in those three weeks Wes was in the hospital, we had to bring in hospice. I didn't want to face that reality, as it actually felt like an out of body experience. I believe that Wes had discussed this with Mark, and then with me that he wanted to be at home and not in the hospital when the inevitable happened. I sort of grasped that, but not totally. Blinders.

Sean told me later that he and Wes had talked. Just the two of them in the hospital, and Wes told him that he wasn't going to make it through the week. He asked Sean if there was anything he wanted to ask him or know, and that it was up to Sean to man up and take care of the family. When Sean told me all of this, it was another gut punch. Wes knew why he was coming home, as did everyone else but me, I was still hanging on to hope. I remember the movie *Hunger Games* when Donald Sutherland says, "The only emotion stronger than fear, is hope." You're stripping me of everything, God, just don't take away my ability to hope. Eventually, even that came to an end.

As Jake had originally wanted to stay home and go to NOVA instead of heading down to Radford for his freshman year in college, his need to show his Dad he had made it to college became paramount. Jake approached me one day about getting down to school for the spring semester, and part of me thought, "You've got to be kidding me." It's not like I didn't have anything else going on. But as I was coming to understand Jake's nondisclosure and tight-lipped emotions, I knew I had to let him go. I discussed it with Wes in the hospital, and he said, "Sharon, Jake will deal with my illness a lot better down at school." I'm not sure if I totally believed that but was so happy to have Wes make that decision and give me his sound advice and feedback. So I progressed with all the details of getting Jake down to Radford for the start of the spring semester. Wes was still in the hospital when it was time for Jake to head down. I was going to drive him down because I wanted to, but also because there had to be some normalcy for our youngest child who was watching his father die and heading off to college for the first time. As Jake came up to the hospital the night before we were leaving, he bent down and gave Wes a hug and a kiss goodbye and grasped his hand and said, "Stay strong Pops." Gut punch on every level. So hard. I remember feeling like I was watching from afar and not grasping what was actually unfolding in front of me, but the truth is, I was actually grasping it, and it was killing me.

Mark talked with me outside Wes' room one day in one of the family lounge areas that the friends and family of Wes Neff had resided for the better part of three weeks. He told me that we needed to take Wes home in an ambulance, and half incredulous, I said, "Wes isn't going home in an ambulance." Mark said, "Sharon, what if there is traffic or more snow, it will be hard on him, this way, he'll be more comfortable." Still miffed, I silently agreed to change my attitude as we talked with Wes about it and let him decide. But I knew what he would say. And I knew there was no way that Wes Neff was going to let an ambulance bring him home, to his house, and carry him inside. It just wasn't going to happen. So I did what any logical, unhinged wife would do in this situation. I presented both sides to Wes and let him decide. And just as I thought, Wes said exactly what I knew he would. No way. No ambulance.

So we scheduled Wes to be discharged on a Friday morning, and Sean, Kara, Wes' sisters Donna and Emily, Mark and I were there to get him home. While I got him dressed in his regular clothes, the nurses that had been taking care of him for the past several weeks came in to see him. I remember one of his nurses coming in by herself and squatting down in front of Wes as he sat on the edge of his bed, and she held his hands and told him to take care of himself. She seemed solemn, as did Wes, but it was heartfelt and she seemed sad. Part of me thought it was odd, but only in the sense that I knew she was saying goodbye to my husband. But I only sort of knew this. I only sort of grasped it. It was all too much to take in and I kept thinking in another part of my brain, "Hey, what's everybody doing and why is everybody acting like this?" I was half transitioning into the reality of our situation, but I was going kicking and screaming.

I brought a blanket and pillows in the car for Wes so he would be comfortable on the ride home, but he wanted no parts of them. He also did not want to sit up in the front seat, but opted for the back seat. Donna sat up front with me.

As we all caravanned back to our house, we drove down Route 50, heading west. I remember watching Wes in my rear view mirror, and as weak as he was, he never once laid down, never leaned over against the side of the car, or leaned back for support, but instead, sat straight up looking at everything that he passed. All the familiar things that he had come to know and experience in his fifty-four years of living in Northern Virginia. I remember watching him and thinking to myself, is he thinking that this is the last time he will ever be on Route 50? Or is this the last time he will pass Prosperity Avenue? Did he think of the million times he had been over to his buddie's house, the brothers Big Bells and Smokey, nicknames for Mike and Sean respectively, as we passed Cedar Lane? Did he think about Arties, at Fairfax Circle, when it used to be Fritzbies, and where we first met, did he think about that? As I continued to drive and watch my husband in the mirror, I also couldn't help but grasp the magnitude of strength this wonderful man possessed as he undoubtedly knew where he was driving to, and why. How? This memory always gives me such pride but also such agony as I imagine what he was going through and what he must have been thinking. But as Wes started, continued through, and ended, he possessed a strength and grace that I was so blessed to witness, as he taught me more lessons than I could ever count in my lifetime. Could I ever possess all that Wes encompassed? I think not. I know not, in fact. He was the strongest person I've ever met. God, let me live forever in the spirit of Wesley.

Four

In those last few weeks that Wes was in the hospital, I would help him shower and get cleaned up. I remember a couple of times, Wes almost seemed embarrassed to have me see how his body now resembled just a shell of his former self. I always felt no matter what that he was wonderful and beautiful and I wanted him to know that always, no matter what. True, Wesley had lost a lot of weight and looked ill, but he still had those broad shoulders that I was still convinced could handle anything. My impression of Wes was never that of a sick man, but always as the still and forever invincible man that I married. Don't get me wrong, I knew how sick he was, but he was still, in my mind, larger than life and still capable of the most amazing things.

In those last few days in the hospital before he came

home, Wes had told me that when he got home, all he wanted to do was take a hot bath in our tub. We both were big bath takers, always. Wes would come home from work and take a hot, hot bath and just relax, and I'd come up and sit on the side and we'd talk about our day and tell stories. Funny how that was just a routine for us. I liked to take mine right before getting into bed. Baths were just something that soothed both of us and calmed us down. When the cancer was progressing, Wes would often take three or four hot baths in a day, often times getting up in the middle of the night to draw a bath and get in and just help the pain, which I suspect was both physical and emotional. I would get up to check on him, and he wasn't in there to talk about the day, but I wanted him to know I was with him, no matter what.

The day we brought him home from the hospital, I made him wait in the car until Sean and I could help him in and straight up the stairs to our room. We got him out of the car, and with one of us on either side of him, Wes Neff walked into his front door, shoulders back, head up and proud, for what would be the last time. We came inside and we all looked at the stairs, as they were daunting to all of us. We asked Wes if he wanted to sit, and he said no, and pointed his finger to just keep going. Sean and I helped him up the stairs, and it took every ounce of strength that still resided in his body to propel him up those steps. All testament to the drive of the human spirit. Determined and strong.

Wesley never stopped letting us know that this was his

way, and he was going to go out the way he wanted to. So up we went with Sean and I working harder the higher we ascended. We got to the top and into our room and sat Wes on the side of the bed. Knowing he was coming home, I had changed all the sheets so he could just sink right in. As the journey home and the walk up the stairs took so much out of him I asked if he just wanted to get into bed and we'd get his bath later. He was adamant about taking it then. I had him stay on the bed as I rushed to get the bath started, then helped him into it as he lowered himself down into the hot water that was always the most relaxing place for him, and the most familiar to both of us. These baths became more commonplace as the cancer progressed. It soothed and calmed him and gave him a temporary relief from the pain and distress. In those crazy moments, it almost seemed like normal times for us. So, as I always did, I sat on the side of the tub and we talked and I helped him wash his hair with the blue plastic Solo cup that he would use if and when he didn't dunk himself down to rinse his hair. He looked at me and said he was ready to get out. I believe that he was also ready to go, as I have thought about those moments over the last many years. I told him to sit tight and I would get Sean to help me get him up and out. I ran to the top of the stairs and called for Sean to come up and help and when I got back into the bathroom, Wes had already gotten himself up and out of the tub. Determined. I was so taken aback and when Sean came up behind me we both shook our heads in disbelief that he was able to hoist himself up to get himself out. He was really weak at this point, but still calling the shots.

I got him dressed and walked him to our bed. I pulled back the covers, and he climbed in. What I remember so vividly was a sense of peace that seemed to encapsulate him. It was obvious that this was where he wanted to be and he wanted his family to be with him when his time came. I remember thinking how all the stress seemed to leave his body and his face as he climbed into his bed and burrowed into his covers to allow what was going to happen. Wesley did get up several times in those next few days to use the bathroom, but he never left our bedroom again. Except for good.

We had a revolving door of Goons that Mark had scheduled to come over and say goodbye. Again, I didn't quite grasp it when one of the goons would sob and hold me and apologize for not being stronger for me. That part of my brain still said, "Hey, what's going on, why are you sobbing?" But I also knew I was refusing to let reality come up for air and present itself and confront me like a bad dream. But as I witnessed all of Wes' best buddies coming over and traveling from far away to see him and say goodbye, it was hardly an occurrence that I could ignore, albeit still trying. Losing Wesley was not just hard on me and the kids, it was hard on everybody. Wes touched and affected so many people and it wasn't just the kids and I losing our strength and our compass, it was the Goons, and all of our other friends and family. I remember when one of the Goons flew in to see Wes. I took him upstairs and I woke Wes up. I said, "Wesley, look who's here. Dave came from Ohio to see you." Wes did wake up and you would have thought he was seeing Dave at a bar or at the Goon Open. He turned his head and got that smile on his face and raised his hand up and said, "Hey man, how are you doing?" I was so amazed at his rally, but of course, watching another friend come to say goodbye was starting to affect my psyche. I was being forced to acknowledge all that I was trying not to. I loved those guys for coming and being there for Wes. I loved them for being there for us, but I loved them the most for loving Wesley with a vengeance.

Early on a Sunday morning, the doorbell rang and as I answered it, a black cloak was standing right at my door. What the heck? It was our parish priest and my sister was with him. Meg had decided that our priest needed to come and see Wes and give him his last rites. I was partly miffed at the suggestion, but also relieved because I was not handling anything administratively on our behalf at all. Everyone else that had taken up residence on our street, were the ones handling it all. So I let them in, and the kids and I along with Wes' sisters followed him upstairs to Wes' bedside. I woke Wes up and said, "Wesley, look who's here, it's Father O'Neil, he wants to give you a blessing." Wes again rallied enough to say hi with a smile on his face. Unbelievable. But as Father O'Neil progressed, he asked Wes if he wanted to convert to Catholicism? I was holding the kids hands and thinking, "Oh no, this isn't going to be good." Wes believed in God, of course he did, but never considered converting. I wasn't' quite sure how this would play out, in our home, in our bedroom, with our parish priest asking if he wanted to convert. I stayed out of it, as did all of us, and Wesley actually raised his head a bit off the pillow and scanned the room. I could only imagine what he was thinking and what he was going to say. It was anybody's guess. But he lowered his head back down and looked straight at Father O'Neil and said he wanted to. It was actually quite a beautiful thing, and in the end, gave me some solace. As Father O'Neil continued to give Wes his last rites, we all stood around the bed in tears, holding onto each other for dear life, as we also knew what this meant. As he continued and then finished, I walked him to the door and he kept telling me what a blessed soul Wes was. When I say Father almost seemed giddy about this encounter, I mean he seemed joyful. I said, "Father, we are still praying for a miracle." He said, in his thick Irish accent, "Darlin' the miracle is happening, he's going home to be with the Lord." He said it several times and again told me how Wes was such a blessed soul. He seemed lighter for it, and affected by the experience. As Meg drove him back to the rectory, he couldn't stop talking about Wes and what a blessed soul he was and how honored he felt to be the one to be there with him and for him. I always knew Wes was a special person, so full of goodness, so full of love and so selfless. Maybe I wasn't totally surprised by Father's reaction, but I only see that stuff in movies, not in my own house.

As the days progressed, all the kids slept in our room with us, to be together, to be with Wes and to help me, help Wes, if he needed anything during the night. Kara slept in the bed with Wes and I, while Jake slept on a mattress and Sean slept on our chair. Any time Wes needed to get up or to use the bathroom, we all jumped up to help.

We had hospice with us and they were there constantly. Emily and Donna stayed at the house for the week, while Marcia and Wes' older brother Eddie and his wife Lori came back and forth daily. Laurie and Nancy packed their bags and showed up without a plan, other than to just be there for me, for Wes, and for us in whatever capacity we needed. I never asked any of them to be there, they just were and I was grateful, because I could not handle anything extra than what was happening right in front of me.

I remember being in the kitchen and hearing something upstairs in my room. I ran upstairs to find Kara and Sean half carrying Wes to the bathroom. They had gotten him into the room but as I came in I stopped them and said to them, "You guys, it's okay, Dad has a diaper on." Wes was lucid in a nanosecond and he whipped his head towards me and put up his fist. I had a gazillion emotions and sensory experiences all going on simultaneously as I watched Wes dictate his life, take charge, and yet the anger on his face was something for the record books. He said, "What do you mean I have a diaper on?" I said, "Wesley, Edwin, put one on you this morning." I thought he really might punch me for the first and only time in our marriage. With a burst of energy, anger and determination, Wes reached down in his pants and with Hulk like force pulled that diaper off and threw it on the bathroom floor. Kara, Sean, and I didn't know if we should start crying, applauding, or ducking for cover. I loved every minute of that display. Well sort of. I really thought he might hit me. He was so angry, it was scary and liberating all at the same time. But Wes had always said that the day he couldn't wipe his own ass was the day he checked out. He let us all know that for the past thirty years and when it truly came down to it, he meant every word of it. Way to go Wes: you are the most amazing person I know. Write your own script on how this is going to play out. And that he did.

I was spending most of my time up in our room with Wes. There was a constant stream of activity in our room but also in the house. The kids would try to retreat from having so many people around and would all three go and hide out in the basement just trying to cocoon themselves and have a few minutes to grasp the enormity of what was going on.

I had called Jake the Friday we brought Wes home from the hospital and told him he needed to come home for the weekend to see Dad. He had only been at school for two weeks. He came in on Saturday and I am pretty sure he just wanted to run and hide instead of watching what was happening. I was so happy to see him when he got home. He would stick around but then head out with his buddies. It was all too much for him to grasp, and the house was full of so many people, it made it more difficult for him to adjust to this on his own terms.

As Tuesday arrived, Wes was not coming around much, and I finally had to acknowledge to myself what was happening in front of me, in spite of my objections, prayers, pleas, and hopes. The fact that I was losing hope tortured me, as it signified my giving up on Wes and that I had totally lost the battle to save him or help and that I had just plain failed. I had an absence of hope, so God even found a way to steal that away from me.

By Wednesday, I instinctively stayed in the bed with Wes almost all day. I had the TV on and I was reading something, I don't even know, but I was right next to him all day. I'm not sure what I knew or how, but I just sensed it was happening. I would come downstairs every once in a while, or when they would get on me to come down and eat, but then went right back upstairs and got into our bed, still trying to imagine our lives as normal and in happier times. Make believe. It doesn't always work out for you but it's not a bad frame of mind when you need it.

They called me to come and eat dinner, and I went down and had a few bites. I think I was downstairs for thirty minutes or so, but went right back up. I came in the room and I immediately knew that it was here, it was upon us. I went to the top of the stairs and I called down to the kids and said, "You guys need to come up here, it's happening." I could tell the second I got back into our room that Wes' breathing had changed and I knew what we were going to be embarking on. The kids all came up, as did Wes' three sisters, while Nancy and Laurie sat on the top of the stairs out in the hall for hours, crying and holding on to each other as they listened to what was happening inside our bedroom.

As the kids and I laid on the bed with Wes, we told him it was okay to go, that it was time. I knew that as much as I didn't want to say it, that I had to let him go and go peacefully. Wesley passed away that Wednesday night at 10:50 p.m. with all of us with him. "It's what every man dreams of Sharon, that when it's their time, their family will be there surrounding them." These are the words of my older brother as he and his wife came over to see us the next day. Kiernan's words have stuck with me ever since and maybe I garner some peace knowing that Wes knew we were all there with him, as his long hard battle with cancer was coming to an end. Go, and be at peace, finally and again Wesley, it is what I want for you. I love you.

I called my sister to tell her and have her call everyone else in the family, and I told Marcia to call Mark so that he could call all the Goons. Everyone did what they needed to do, as we waited for the hospice nurse to come and pronounce the time of death.

After Wes passed, Sean got up from the bed and went into the hall and told Nancy and Laurie to come in and help me. They did, but I didn't know until later that he had done that. As we waited, Mark drove all the way back over, and as he came into the room, he went up to Wesley, and got on the bed and laid right next to him and held him tight and told him, it was okay, you are not in pain anymore. It was one of the most beautiful things I've ever been witness to. Thank you Mark for showing me what it means to love a friend.

When we came back into the kitchen, Laurie insisted that Kara and I take an Ambien. What the hell is that? I had no idea and wanted no part of it. She swore it would help us sleep and I said I had Tylenol PM, and didn't need any of that other stuff but she insisted. She said we would sleep and not feel groggy the next morning. As I continued to resist and she continued to extol its virtues, I took one and as Kara and I went back up to our room, I started walking into the door jambs, although I felt lucid, except for the immense pain that was in my heart, but I felt like a noodle and kept saying, "Kara, what is this stuff she just gave us?" I got into bed and slept the whole night and have been taking Ambien ever since. It's not something I'm proud of and certainly for someone who takes nutrition and supplements and believes in a more natural way for health, I couldn't discount the immense relief that Ambien provided. You have to turn the grief off sometime, you have to turn the pain off sometime. It's all just too much. If I didn't have Ambien, I would be awake all night crying, thinking, and losing my mind. You have to turn off the grief, and Ambien has been my vehicle for that to happen. I quickly realized though that although I took whatever Laurie gave me that night, I needed to pay attention to the amount. For those first few nights, we still had a revolving door in our house and on Friday night, the Goons showed up with kids in tow and a lot of American Honey, one of Wes' favorite liquors. So as they all came around to cocoon us and help us walk this difficult walk, we ended up with many that drank a lot. Most of the kids did, so I was told. As I went to bed with my Ambien, Jake came in around 2:00 a.m. and wanted to talk. He was pretty hammered, but he was in the mood to talk. If Jake wants to talk, you better believe I am going to listen. The problem for me this night is that I had taken an Ambien, still having no idea what the milligrams were. As Jake came to the side of my bed and kneeled down, I was forcing myself awake to talk with him. He said "Mom, I'm okay with this and Dad, because I've got Dad's blood running through my veins and that's all good." I remember trying to grasp the enormity of what he was saying to me and thinking how profound he was as I was so thankful for his words. They impacted me then, and continue to do so.

As Jake and I continued to have our heart to heart, the rest of the house was in chaos. Apparently the kids took the bourbon down to the basement and had their own party of which there were several that were toasted, along with my kids but one of Jake's buddies was getting sick. He had wedged himself into the powder room and pulled out the vanity drawer, which inhibited the door from being opened. As he was on the floor getting sick, he assumed that was the optimal time to call his girlfriend up in Boston. Perfect timing, I'd say. What every girl wants to hear, but as that was going on Sean was trying to get Johnny out of the bathroom but couldn't get the door opened. He came up to my room and said, "Jake come here." Jake walked over and Sean told him what was going on with his buddy who was locked in the bathroom. Unconcerned, Jake let Sean handle it and came back to talk with me. In the end, Sean was able to get the drawer closed and get Johnny downstairs with a trashcan after first hanging up on the girlfriend. It is amazing how life keeps going right along while you are in the midst of the tragedy.

Five

Funeral arrangements are upon us. It's one of the most disturbing and surreal experiences in the world, in your life, especially when you are in charge of arranging it. Most everyone around me has been laying out the outline for what needs to be done and then telling me, and we go and do it. I make decisions, in a way. We go to the church and pick out the readings and the songs I want sung. I know that I want "On Eagles Wings" sung as well as "Ave Maria." That is about the only thing I am sure about.

Eddie, Nancy, and I go back to the funeral home to go over the details, and pick out the Mass card. I pick the one that says "Grieve Not." I pick it because I know that is what Wes would be saying to all of us.

If I should ever leave you, whom I love, to go along the silent way, grieve not. Nor speak of me with tears, but laugh and talk of me as if I were beside you there. And when you hear a song or see a bird I loved, please do not let the thought of me be sad. For I am loving you just as I always have. There are so many things I wanted still to do, so many things to say to you. Remember I did not fear. It was just leaving you that was so hard to face.

Grieve Not. But I do, and I will forever.

Before leaving we have to see Wes, before cremation. Nancy doesn't want me to go in. She wants Eddie to do it, but I will have absolutely no part of that. I have to confirm that it is indeed Wes, and so we all go in. It is so difficult to see him there, but there is no way I'm not going to see this through until the end. I will not leave you Wes, ever, no matter how hard it is on me. And so I do confirm, that it is in fact, my husband.

We have to pick out flowers and clothes to wear. We have to get pictures together for the video, we have to get the music together that I want to accompany the video. I can hardly believe all this is going on. I don't even know how or who is doing it. I just simply can't absorb anymore. Our friends and families are amazing. They just take over and handle everything for us, as it should be. We have to decide where to have the reception. I say at the house, but Laurie and Nancy don't think it would hold everyone so we decide on a reception hall, where we rent a room and will have all the food prepared.

We have tons of people around, which I am happy for, as we go about the task of trying to prepare for the wake and the funeral. We have the wake so that we can eulogize Wes, because in the Catholic Church the priest says the eulogy. We all know that we want to have all his friends and family up there to tell stories and share all the special things about him that we all deserve to hear, and all that we cherish about him.

As we get to the funeral home for the wake, the video is playing on a continuous loop. Somehow I missed the specifics of this, but that is why other people take charge at times like these. There were all these great pictures of Wes with all the music I had picked out and somehow it didn't register with me, but there it was, my husband up on the big screen playing our music. I watch as the kids go into the room and sit in a pew. As I watch them, my heart breaks again and again. I go back out to the reception area and a line is forming and I start greeting people and then the line grows longer and longer and I am there, receiving all the people that loved Wes. It is hard to stand there, as I am so worried about the kids and oddly, all the people that come to say goodbye to Wes and are at a loss, just like us.

I remember standing there and looking around the room for Waz. He was younger than Wes, by a year, but they had been friends since they were six years old. Waz was heartbroken and I guess I never realized how much Wes was Waz's idol. So I was worried about him and I wanted to find him in the crowd and check on him, but I saw him in a corner, and I suspected he was staying as close to the wall with the insulation of all the other Goons, because this was just too hard. I wanted to get to him and give him a hug. Who knows, that may have been even harder for him, but I remember so vividly that he was the one I was so worried about. I never got to see him and give him a hug until much later.

When we go into the chapel for the eulogies, I tell Mark that I want to go first. I am steeling myself to get through this eulogy for Wes, because I want to do it for him. I want everyone to know what I knew, what we knew, about what a great person he was. And so Mark walks up to the podium to address the room and let them know what the plan is. I go up and am able to give my husband's eulogy without a total melt down. That in and of itself is monumental. I want to tell Wes' story for everyone to hear and to share more about him. I want them to know what I know. What the kids know also. How do you tell a story about one of the greatest people you've ever known and were lucky enough to love and be loved by? I want to do him justice.

Wes was the one that brought the love and the laughter into our home. His unconditional love of all of us was the cornerstone of our family. I kept the calendar and the schedules but Wes brought all the good stuff. None of us wanted to disappoint him, although that was tough to do, because he didn't disappoint easily. Without pushing or dictating, we all just wanted to be like him. He was so special.

As I finished my eulogy, four of the Goons got up to speak. Kevin, Greek, Pest, and Smokey. It proved to be difficult so Smokey told all of the Goons to come up to the stage and stand together. And so they did, about twenty of them, all in solidarity of each other, but also for the love of their best buddy. The stories were great, and I loved having all of them up there. It warmed all of our hearts to witness a group of guys that are there for each other with no questions asked and they too, loved each other completely and utterly unconditionally. What a gift the Goons have and continue to give, to all of us.

As we wrapped up the Wake, I was taken aback at the number of people there for Wes. It was evident again and again, how many people he touched. Wesley was such a good and pure soul. How can he be gone? Is this really happening?

As we girded ourselves to get through the actual funeral, we were all exhausted. It was all coming down pretty hard on us, as the finality was hitting us and setting in for the long haul. Once we got through the formalities of the funeral, we were faced with the reality that Wes was no longer here. As everyone packed up to go back and reengage in their lives, we were sitting here trying to figure out what the hell happened. What do we do now? How do we live? How do we approach the next day, and then the next? For God's sake, somebody give us a playbook.

As luck would have it, my father had a heart attack and was put into ICU the same day Wes died. I could only handle one thing at a time and what was going on inside my house was pretty intense. The day after Wes died, I drove to the hospital and walked down the corridors of yet another hospital to go and see my dad. He was confused and I had to tell him again that Wes had passed away. He was so sad, but equally sad that he couldn't pull that information up into his memory on his own. I wanted to run. I wanted to run out the doors and never come back, of course I did, but I didn't, until I could, but even then, I couldn't run too far, because Act II was ramping up. That was the constant care of my father, bridled with unprecedented grief over the loss of my husband.

Six

There is nothing in this world like the finality of death. There just isn't. No matter how much we all realize how this game is going to end, we are never fully prepared for its consequences. We are all raised to know that there will be an end one day. But no matter how much you can reason that within yourself, even spiritually, you are never prepared enough for that finality. You just aren't. It is like a shock wave through your system, one that's hard to reconcile. When Wes died, we still had people around us thankfully. There was the funeral to arrange, and actually get through; there were familial issues to be taken care of, and I was thankful for being in shock, a byproduct of grief, and letting that be my insulator, until it wasn't anymore. And then I was hit again, maybe even worse than I was when Wes first died.

It was about a week after Wes passed away that Kara, Sean and I went to lunch with Wes' sisters. Things were starting to hit me, but it wasn't until after lunch, when we got back to the house, that I lost it all. I came up to my room to change and I ended up in our closet and became totally unhinged, out of my mind, and absolutely could not control any part of my emotions. I think I was trying to be quiet, but I was found. In the closet. First, by Kara, then by Sean, then by Wes' sister Donna. We were all in the closet, on the floor, with all of Wes' clothes and his laundry basket that held the last clothes ever to be worn by him. We were all there, coming apart at the seams and the reality that Wes wasn't there, was coming home to roost in our heads and hearts more than we were prepared to handle. The finality was hitting me. I can't handle this, I am not going to make it. The pain is just too much. The pain and agony actually got worse, much worse, as I quickly discovered.

Our collective time in the closet, on Wes' side, was a starting point for me, as I tend to gauge the degree to which I am falling apart based on my first night in the closet. I remember the kids coming in to get me, and they dropping to the floor beside me and in front of me, to hold me, and cry with me. No judgments, just the unconditional love and support of the same kids that just lost their father and now were watching their mother crumble to the floor, writhing under the magnitude of pain that was now to become the barometer during the ensuing days, months, and years. The kids never tried to sugar coat my pain and grief, nor their own, but instead always allowed me to cry and feel all that I was feeling. On saner days and times, I would contemplate if it was fair to do all of this to them, or if I shouldn't try to hide the pain and hold it all in. The truth of the matter was, that even on my best day or my stronger moments, I was not even remotely able to hold anything in. I just couldn't. When I say I had no energy to be strong, I mean, there was none.

There were days where I was so depleted that I could barely muster getting out of bed. As I clearly made conscious decisions to never stay in bed, getting up and out of the bed was a laborious chore. The difficulty became always: what am I getting up for? The vapid hours of the day ahead dangled in front of me, taunting me to try to hit it head on, but without the energy to do so. I am thankful for the Ambien that I was taking, because it was the only way I could fall asleep, and falling asleep wasn't even the main reason for taking my wonderful sleeping aid. The fact was and still is, that I had to be able to turn this pain and grief off sometime. If I didn't have Ambien, I would be up all night crying and thinking that I wanted to die myself, right there alongside Wes. Even in the light of day, I had to deal with those same thoughts, but the nighttime, in the dark, in the quiet and solitude of just myself, was so grim, so hard and seemingly unforgiving and morbidly unrelenting.

One of the Goons asked me one time what the hardest part of the day was. He assumed it was falling asleep. I said it was getting up. I had the luxury of Ambien to put me out, but I had no luxury upon waking up. As I started to stir in the morning, all the memories flooded in, the same ones that had been waiting on the doorstep of my mind throughout the night, but not been allowed to enter because of medications. They came rushing in and reminded me immediately of what I had lost and what I was supposed to conquer. But you need drive to conquer, don't you? Truly, I didn't want to conquer anything. I had no goals in mind. No plan of attack to get me from one day to the next, and in my case, nothing to get me from one moment to another. The mornings were excruciating as I often woke up crying, even without the benefit of opening my eyes. The tears were always there. Always. Some of the hardest days, moments and mornings for me were when, upon awakening, I had to acknowledge that I was alone. I was without Wes. I immediately had to contemplate how in God's name I was going to get through this day, and how, how I was going to get from 6:00 a.m. to midnight. What was I going to put in my day to help me through? How would I find anything to distract me or help me to keep walking? These became constant, calculating and conscience thoughts on my part, every day, but without the energy to execute. This daily grind was pure torture for me. On most days, it took all of my energy to just get up and get out of bed. Think about what it would be like to have nothing in front of you for the day. No goal, no objective, just an empty void. That was pretty much how everyday played out for me, and it seemed like I was living a slow death. There was literally nothing to look forward to, nothing that I could "feel" anything about. That's what it is like to feel dead inside.

I started to learn new techniques to get me through the nighttime ritual of falling asleep and of waking up. The TV was my lifeline. As I still do to this day, I fell asleep with the TV on. I took a cat nap, then woke up and took my Ambien and turned off the TV. I have switched from the late night news programs to watching reruns of "Friends," and "Modern Family." I am pretty adamant that I fall asleep with funny stuff swirling in my brain instead of the heavy stuff that is always residing in me. I hated when I would wake up and the TV was still on at one or two in the morning. That seemed wrong and always screamed to me of how diabolical this grief and pain is and how it was wreaking havoc in my life. A constant reminder of how off my life really was or is. So as the TV was the distraction at night, it became my distraction for rising in the morning also. It took me a little while to come to this conclusion and find a solution to my pained mornings, but not before I had a million mornings of crying for Wes in my sleep, and wanting so desperately to start the day with him. I would often replay what our day would be and how it would start. I'd try to pretend that Wes was right there in the bed with me, or up and getting ready to go get his coffee and say hi to the world. I would try to replay what our conversations would be early in the morning, even while it was still dark outside and before the alarm would go off. My alarm, that is, because Wes' alarm was in his head. I don't know if he ever set a real alarm, but up he would be, on time, no matter what crazy hour he needed to be. Reliving the life and the moments of the life you still yearned for and crave, is daunting. I would think about the early mornings where Wes would start to awaken and he would reach over and pull me across the bed and in close to him and just hold me. It was the greatest gift to wake up to, and so I would wake up and always be thankful. Thankful to be waking up wrapped in the arms of the greatest person I knew and loved. To be sure, being in Wes' arms and being in his life was the safest, greatest place I had. How great is that? I long for those moments every day. As the mornings got harder and harder for me to reconcile, I started to turn on the TV the second I started to wake up. It became the greatest distraction for me immediately. I would have Wes in my head and heart but watching the morning news was in the forefront of my mind and somehow I was able to get out of bed and actually start the day. I had my IPod in the bathroom and that would get turned on also. Distractions, the great equalizer in grief and despair.

People keep telling me that it will get easier with time. But it doesn't. It's a lie, by the way. At least for me. Now, I can go longer periods without tears when I'm distracted, but then I get a sucker punch to the gut and I'm slammed with the reality that Wes isn't here. When this happens, and all the time when it happens, it brings me to my knees and then I have to deal with this immense guilt. Why do I get to be out here having lunch at some restaurant, or shopping and looking for stupid stuff, and Wes isn't able to? The guilt of still living. It haunts me every day and never lets me out of its clutches. It's the great tormentor to be sure, and one that never seems to go away. Will it ever? I can hardly stand it.

I had a meltdown again. No one was at home and I felt so alone. The kids were at work and Jake was out of town. I sat on the floor sobbing, but first I walked around in circles, crying. I miss him so much. The foreverness of this hits me again and again. I want him back. I want a do-over. God, please give me another chance to get this right. I beg of You, God, even though I don't believe in You anymore.

I spent fifteen months trusting in God. I spent every waking hour saying prayers. Prayers that were not new to me. I've always said them and have always had a very deep faith. God has always been paramount to my daily living. Until now.

I bought into all of the rhetoric. "Believe in Him and He will see you through." Give up your burdens…all nonsense. But I believed it, until it turned out not to be true. The fact is, that I truly believed God would see us through. I believed this with everything in me. But what I believe to have been utter torture for Wes for the sixteen months that he was sick is what I can't forgive God for. So I try to continue on in a life where the two greatest anchors of my life are now gone: Wes and my faith. I've lost the major forces in my life. Both of those were in my heart and soul always, until it wasn't. And I now have nothing.

People ask me how I'm doing and I say, "I suck." I'm not in anyone's face with this answer, I don't have the energy to be in anyone's face about anything. But it is just a fact, and I can't sugar coat it for anyone. It might make some people uncomfortable, but I am in this shit show and that is just the way it is. It sucks, all the way around. I don't even have the energy to put on a good show. I'm not okay, I am so not okay. How am I supposed to pretend?

Wes leaving was the worst thing ever. Again, who is ever truly prepared for a death? Sure, I could speculate about what it would be like if Wes died, and that scene in my mind wasn't too great, of course it wasn't, but my reality was worse than any of my worst fears. As I go through each day, it physically hurts me to not be able to touch him, kiss him, smell him and see him. I never got tired of looking at Wes. He was the most beautiful man I have ever seen. Every time I caught a glimpse of him, my heart skipped. He took my breath away every day.

This new life that I have to walk now is so hard and I don't want any part of this single life. I loved being married and I loved being married to Wes. It was a gift and it was fun. I don't want to do this. I love you Wes. I want to write it on a card again. I want to say it out loud to him and have him respond, hopefully smile. I want to leave him a message on his voicemail. Oh yea, I already do, I still do. I listen to his voicemail message to hear his voice and then I cry. I cry all over again. I leave messages begging him to come home. Please come home Wes, I miss you. Please God, let me have a do-over.

I'm sitting on the floor of my bedroom staring at a 16x20 picture of Wes that was printed for his memorial service. I'm crying. What else? It's 4:00 on a Wednesday afternoon and all I want to do is crawl into a hole and go away. I can't take any more of this. I'm short of breath. I really think I'm cracking up. I have no motivation and everything is an effort. A huge effort. Another sucker punch. Life's reality that it will never be as good as it was. Never as joyful; never as happy. It is crazy being in this state of mind. I literally feel like I am in a lifeboat in the middle of the ocean with no land in sight and no rudder. I'm just floating, going nowhere. It's so dismal. I have no hope. God stripped me of all hope and even worse yet, my ability to ever hope again.

I am hit by the fleeting thought that maybe I didn't want to see the alternative to Wes' illness. But who would? As if admitting to the severity of Wes' illness would have better prepared me for this onslaught of pain. It wouldn't. I can't live without Wes and I don't want to, but I must. We have three beautiful kids and Wes would never forgive me if I gave into this. But there are days that it's all I want to do. Like today. My obligation to the kids overpowers me, and my distress. But some days they are competing emotions. Today I don't know which way to turn and my stomach hurts. I don't want to eat today. I've got to pick myself up and move. Just move Sharon. Fight, try to fight, just for a few hours. Try. But the fight is gone. It was all used up fighting for Wes. My energies were never better spent, but my efforts weren't realized. This whole scene blows and I hate it.

I wonder if I will ever think happy or manageable thoughts again. I don't see it but everyone tells me it will happen. They tell me you just have to walk it and go through it. You'll come out on the other side. I say, the other side is without my best friend and my playmate, there will be no happiness. It's what I think, anyway.

I feel like I weigh a thousand pounds today. That's how much grief weighs, a thousand pounds. I can barely shuffle my feet to move. Some days I shed some of those pounds, but only briefly. Some days I only shed them for a moment or an hour, but the weight always comes back on. I was at my Dad's house last night to sit with him because of his heart issues. I walked in and my sister was there at the table with him and I asked how he was doing and how his blood pressure was today. He got terse with me and snapped that why was I asking those questions and I was just being nosey. I sat there stunned, and in absolutely no shape to take the Colonel's abuse. But I got this picture of Wes in my head and thought about how he would have handled this or what would he have done if he were here to witness this exchange. Wes would have made one of his goofy faces and smiled or said something that would have broken the ice. I would still have been wounded but he would have comforted me. Instead, I had to go to the bathroom and cry because he wasn't there and I had to deal with more bullshit alone. More than I could handle, by the way. I wanted to bolt. Screw the Colonel. He shouldn't have been so nasty to me and Wes should have been there to make me feel better. That's the way it always worked. Wes shielded me from my family and was always my safety net. Now, all I have is the bathroom.

Two weeks ago, my Dad was in the hospital for more heart issues and it wasn't looking good. We set up a meeting with Evercare and met with the hospice nurse. My whole family was there for the meeting. Being my Dad's executor and POA, I literally had to sign all of the same papers for my father as I just did for Wes six weeks prior. Did I really look like someone who can take this kind of stress? Looks are deceiving. It had all been too much. Then for my Dad to give me a hard time that night…I'm really done. I'm crawling in a hole. Good night Irene.

It's been seven weeks since Wes died. It's Saturday and I am supposed to go to my Dad's to sit for a couple of hours to relieve my one sister and wait for the other. They all have been taking over the responsibilities of my dad to give me some time, but I try to help out where I can. But it isn't easy. Not even a little bit. I woke up and couldn't get the heaviness out of my heart. The thousand pounds were back and I wasn't even out of bed yet. I had no desire to get out of bed. I felt so alone and I started crying. Crying keeps me company or so it seems. My new best friend. It was a weird morning. It felt different in a way. I'm not sure if it was because I was going to my Dad's house and that actually stresses me out more. But I had nothing to look forward to, although these days that all seems relative. I don't look forward to much, except Ambien.

So the crying started in bed. I got up and went into the bathroom and cried some more. I got dressed and put on some makeup and couldn't get out of the closet. I was sitting on Wes' side of the closet, holding all of his clothes. I still hadn't washed anything. I was on his chair crying and smelling his clothes and ended up on the floor. I tried to catch my breath, but I thought it could all end right there for me. I had no strength and no fight. I'm fought out. I got nothing. It's amazing how you can cry and cry and after a while, your mind shifts to something else. I guess our minds need to take a breather from all the distress. So I got up and put on more mascara and got ready to head to my Dad's. Only problem was the crying came back and I had to deal with that as I made the drive over. What was there to look forward to? My Dad is in congestive heart failure and he is confused. Not sure what will greet me when I get there. Nastiness or complacency? When my sister Patty got there and asked how I was doing, I started crying all over again.

Another bad morning. I've gotten up crying for the last three or four days in a row. I can't move forward. I wake up crying. Yesterday I was cleaning the kitchen and just lost it again. Sean came up and saw me and said, "Mom, what's up?" I couldn't hold it in and I let loose. He hugged me well, as he always does and let me cry as he started crying also. I just don't know what to do with all of this. This grief and pain. These raw emotions. No filter to it – there is no energy to filter it. What you see is what it is a lot of the times. Mostly, in fact.

Today seemed to be a better day. I felt steadier than I have in several days. I realize it is just a matter of time before the hurt gets to be too much again, but I have to store up my reserves to get through the next time. Crying has become a way of life. I can cry without effort or thought these days. When you think about crying, you visualize sobs, but so often the tears literally just roll down my cheeks without the convulsions. When the tears and the convulsions hit, it's sheer hell. I'm living in hell right now.

I came home and went downstairs to see Sean. He was watching a movie and was sad. We talked about Wes and how great he was and how he was proud of him. Sean teared up and all I could do was give him a hug. I hope I hug him as well as he hugs me. I want to shield the kids from all this pain. It hurts as much as it did when I couldn't shield Wes from the pain and hurt. I'd still be fighting for him, if only I could.

Sean told me this week that his friends think that because it's been two months since Wes passed away that he should be over it. He followed with a, "Fuck that." I could tell things were building up in him when he called into work one morning and said he'd be late. He came into the kitchen and asked for eye drops because his eyes were red. I gave him a hug and he lost it. Weeks of sadness came out when he was getting his tie on and saw a picture of Wes, and he couldn't hold it in anymore. It's hard to watch when your kids fall apart. We talked and I tried to tell him that all that Dad gave to him would be a source of comfort for him at some point. Not now, but sometime later. He regrouped and went to work. He sent me a text later thanking me for helping him get through the rough spot and that he felt better letting it all out. I totally get it. We hold it in until we can't anymore and it then it comes out in sobs. Sean gives me strength, Kara gives me support, and Jake gives me hope. Wes would be so proud of them. When the kids and I talk about Wes, we know that he was so much more than what he let on. He was always easy going and unpretentious and definitely understated. He never tooted his own horn and he did so much for people and affected so many just by being so genuine. Wes had been a steady hand for all of us. They are all so much like him but in different ways, and I love seeing Wes' qualities in the three of them. I am so taken aback at how they are sticking close to me and helping me through. They seem to be the steady hand now. I think I am supposed to be there for them. I think they are here for me.

I go to Dad's to help him out. It's my turn. He is Daddy again and I am thankful. I haven't seen that since before Wes died. With all of my dad's issues happening at the same time as Wes dying. It's been tough on my whole family. Although I wasn't there doing very much, I am trying to do a little more now. He has been getting better and better and last night he was talking to me about Wes and about loss. My Mother died in 1980 and my father still misses her, and he never remarried. I've tried to avoid these conversations with my dad because I will cry. Of course I will. And on this night I didn't set out to cry, but of course I do. He is great and just talks with me gently about life. He tells me to be strong and pray that God gives me strength to get me through this. I don't have the heart to tell him I am not speaking to God anymore. It would upset him. But I do tell him that God wasn't there for us and my dad quietly said, "Well Sharon, you don't know how God will reveal to you how he has helped you. It may be in other ways, down the road." Well, okay, but it's not when we needed him. My dad's words have stuck with me, though. Of course they have.

We just passed the three-month mark. I'd never spent more than a week away from Wes since the day I met him. I hate every minute of this. I woke up this morning and listened to his voicemail message on my cell phone. "Hi, this is Wes, I am sorry but I can't come to the phone right now but please leave a message and I'll get back to you as soon as I can, thank you very much. " Happiness in his voice, like there always was. He was amazing. I have his cell phone on my nightstand and look at it every time I come in my room and check to see if anyone has called. A lot of times, it's only me. I check his phone because I just want to see activity on it. I can't close out his account. I listen to his voicemail just to hear his voice. I'd like to say it brings me comfort but in truth it almost hurts too much. I want to see Wes' name show up on my cell screen. I want him to just be out of town and to call me at midnight and whisper how much he loves me. I used to have both phones right next to me when he was away. He'd either call on the house phone or my cell and I wanted to be able to answer quickly. Now, neither of the phones ring.

No one is calling me to tell me that they love me. Not at midnight anyway. It's such a huge void. The attention. Wes always paid attention to me. I don't think I need more than my fair share, but maybe I do. Either way, what Wes gave me, I ate up.

I now realize my bed is big. Too big, in fact. It's funny that when Wes was here, there were nights that it seemed too small, but now it's an ocean. We fell asleep almost every night holding hands. I want to fall asleep tonight holding Wes' hand, but all I can hold onto is his pillow, and I hold on to that for dear life. That, Ambien and the TV. I think again about spending the next thirty years without Wes, and I want to fold. How am I going to do that? It's excruciating to consider this possibility. I just want to hold his hand. I change the sheets on our big ocean bed and no one has been on Wes' side. This hurts my heart in ways you can't even imagine. If I forgot to get the sheets back on the bed before Wes went upstairs for the night, he'd just stare at the bed. I'd come up and he'd help me put the sheets on. Come home Wes, the sheets are clean, our favorite thing. It's time for bed, I'm cold and I need you to keep me warm. I love you and miss you. I am going to get into bed and call your phone and say good night. And so I do. Good night Sweet Wesley.

Seven

This family needs Wes. I am not equipped.

We had a tough week in the sense that Kara accepted a job with Wes' good friend Dave, but the job description seemed to go from one thing to something completely different. This was something Kara wasn't prepared for, and it was causing her a lot of anxiety as to whether she should take it or not. I sat in my closet and cried because I didn't know how to advise her. We would always trust Wes for things like this. I sobbed at my inability to console her or direct her, and for the loss of Wes; the father advising the daughter. Kara cried for Wes also. I felt helpless. I called Greek, another Goon and close friend of Wes' and ours, and asked him for advice since he is in sales also. I cried a lot and he said, "Sharon, I'm gonna tell you what Wes would say: if you're not comfortable with the job, don't take it." He assuaged a lot of fear for me and he called Kara and talked her through it as well. He helped her sort out her emotions about the job and helped her find her voice to say she didn't think she could take the job as it was newly outlined. She called Dave and he was not sure why it was outlined the way it was either, but he too, counseled her and encouraged her to come to the training in Wisconsin, and so she did.

We have been so lucky to have all of the Goons to help prop us up and walk us through. We have been blessed with family, friends, neighbors and Goon love, and we count our blessing every day.

Through all of this, I have learned to accept help. It's not easy. A lot of false pride has always kept me from accepting too much. But these days, it seems as if nothing is too much, because I need all the help I can get. I am truly not equipped to handle all that is coming at me. The kids want Wes, for all the same reasons that I do, but also to be their security blanket, our voice of reason. Wes usually made a lot of the big decisions about the kids. He would support me on decisions I felt were important regarding them, but when the heavy stuff came down, I was always thankful he took the lead. He was always just calmer about it. Without him, we have the Goons to step in and help us all make decisions large and small, and for the moment, it makes us feel like we have a rudder.

Some days I feel like I've sunk. My ship isn't sailing too well. I feel at this point that I am not able to handle life and my kids and being what I should be for them without Wes. I feel like I'm in hell a lot of times. Wes come home. As I try to adjust to these changes that are happening every second of every day in this new world of mine, I am so often caught off guard by another surge of grief and the resounding feeling that I am so inept without him. Aloneness is something I will not get used to because I don't want to. I shouldn't have to, but this is my new life. I feel so alone so much of the time and I hate the feeling of isolation that goes hand in hand with grief. Having these fleeting thoughts about going through the rest of my life without Wes makes me want to throw up, and I almost do. These days, it happens a lot. I want to scream and cry, the thoughts are so overpowering. It is so sad. I have to contemplate doing this life thing without him. But how? How will I ever be able to get through this, if I even want to?

So much of the grieving process is about getting through the day to day but also in actually acknowledging the fact that Wes is gone, and will not be back. I live in this realm of still trying to figure out how I will see him again, or replaying and reliving all the things that we did together on a daily basis. Missing all of that and missing out on those little joys, becomes a monumental task. The utter shroud of sadness weighs a ton. It is no laughing matter. I am tormented by my emotional state and end up sloughing through the hours, days and weeks. As I am conflicted by wanting and yearning to touch him, to hold him and to feel his hand in mine I am also tortured by the realization that this is never going to happen again.

Ever. There I said it. But I don't believe it, or not totally yet, anyway. I play games with myself all the time. I go to the same places, leave at the same time, listen to the same radio channels and try to reenact my life with Wes. How long can this go on? How long can I continue to pretend that my life is still intact on some level and at the same time try to wrap my head around the fact that it is not. It is not the same. Not anymore.

As I play these games with myself, I am also simultaneously having to reconcile this new real life. Reality keeps rearing its ugly head and forcing me to adjust and acknowledge. I have to take care of business. I have to change accounts and send in death certificates and go to the bank and go to the attorney's office and change our will. I have to change it from ours to just mine. I cry at the table. I don't sob, but the tears roll down my face in a constant stream and pool on my lap, or collect at the bottom of my chin. I can't look anyone in the eye, not the estate attorney, not the witness that has been called in to watch me sign the new "mine" document and I can't look at Mark, our friend, one of Wes' best, as well as our accountant, and now my rock. I can't look at him. I can't handle this moment in time. I want to run and get the hell out of that chair, out of that office, and away from that table that holds my new will, with only my name on it. I don't want to take Wes' name off of this document, I don't want to. I scream it as loud as I can, without the luxury of a single sound escaping my pursed lips. No noise comes out. Nothing is audible but the pounding of my heart and the throbbing in my head as I finally make it official. I am now only one.

As this circus in my heart and head is taking place, I am acutely aware that the facilitators of this torture are somewhat tortured themselves. I realize that they realize I'm in turmoil and it is uncomfortable for everyone. Maybe they can empathize with what I am going through. Maybe they are putting themselves in my shoes. Don't do it, don't put yourselves in my shoes, you don't want to feel what I'm feeling. No one should have to feel what I'm feeling. But maybe they do anyway. When we are done, Mark and I shake everyone's hands for the sheer pleasure of the torture they have just put me through, and he and I leave. I make it to the elevator, but just barely. Mark and I don't say a word to each other until we get to the elevator and he gives me a big hug. This hurts him just as much as it hurts me. Wes was one of his best, I know that Wes was mine. I know what he's feeling and I think he has a pretty good sense of what I am feeling. After all, Mark has been with us, at the hospital, at home, pretty much everywhere, and now, he is navigating all the changes that are needed for me to be only one. Widow. Forgive me for saying that it all just sucks. I hate this new life without him. It makes me cry all over again. God, will this ever stop? I'm pretty sure you can drown in your own tears.

Transitioning to this new role of widow and of one is painful. Plain and simple. Grief is a process and with it, a process to healing. In the beginning – you would have never made me believe that healing was coming out of all of this pain, but I guess it is, it does and it has. Reluctantly so, to be sure. The loss of a loved one is immensely intense. I know for me, I always felt better just being with Wes. Just being in his presence made me feel whole. It is difficult to adjust that sense of security one has with another and also with oneself after your loved one dies. It is remarkably hard to counteract these new emotions with the ones that have always been your sense of security. But as we transition into this new life, this is an additional aspect we now have to carry. But as I hate being alone, single, unmarried, and widowed; God I hate that word as much as I hate the state of being, change is coming and I have no choice but to ride the tide.

Four months come around of being a widow. I can hardly believe that I am here to talk about it and still standing. There were so many times I thought I couldn't do it anymore. I just couldn't. But somehow, I took one more step. I try to train myself to get focused and get to work. This is a huge problem. Grief is like having ADD. Focus is a luxury, I quickly come to find out. It is not a given, not anymore. I try to push all my sadness aside and get my head in the game. Just push forward Sharon, just try. This is my new pep talk to myself. Everyday. But I also hate cheerleaders, I've come to realize.

I wake up these days and ask Wes to give me strength. Still not believing that God is in my corner, He doesn't get my prayers or even my acknowledgement, not now and maybe never. That remains to be seen. As for now, Wes gets my prayers, and my begging for mercy. Please Wes, help me. So

I ask Wes to give me strength today instead of wallowing in grief. It seems as if that is all I can do. I don't know how to walk this walk. Wes kept saying these are the cards we've been dealt and we have to deal with it. This hand sucks. Wes, this hand sucks, roll me another please. All of these day-to-day issues need attention. The yard is a mess. I look out the kitchen window and all I see are weeds. They seem to have overtaken the yard. I need to push myself to get out there and work. The yard seems to get bigger and bigger, or maybe I've just gotten smaller and smaller. I do get out in the yard and start the process, but this day is not turning out to be a very good day. I attempt all the work, but the tears are there, everywhere actually. I walk into the garage and I see Wes' Timberland boots. His work boots. In the winter he wore them a lot. I always loved him in those boots. He was rugged and good looking. I lost it on the boots. I could see him in them as they were perfectly molded to his feet. It's just more torture. Can the pain of a broken heart be harder to endure than actual physical pain? I just don't know. I wish I could just take a Tylenol and ease the pain, but when I do, nothing goes away but my headaches. The rest I'm left to deal with.

I get up and have absolutely nothing to look forward to. Isolation is how I feel on this particular day. I need a shrink. I need to make an appointment. It's been about a month and I am screaming for help. What do I do with all of this? It is sheer hell inside my head and my heart. I end up having a meltdown in the shower and I can't get out because I am crying so hard. I have no choice but to stay with it and let it happen. I have to let it out. I actually scream on this day. I scream a lot and I scream loud. Sometimes I hold my hand over my mouth and let it go. I'm scared. I'm scaring myself. It all sounds primal. I am raw emotions. I keep thinking that I am not the strong one, that Wes was, or at least he made me feel strong. Without him, I am weak. I fear that I will be a weak person for the rest of my life. I liked the strength I garnered from being with Wes. But it's not here, not today. Not in this shower. But I allow myself to go with it and feel it all, all the horrid pain of this day, this week, this month. I let it rip. I have no choice. I guess the upshot of this day is that I finally got out of the shower.

Kara and I drive to the beach. She falls asleep on the ride and I start crying. No sobs, just tears. But they are coming down my face. Kara catches me and she gets upset. It hurts her to see me like this. She tells me that it is hard to see me sad like this because she doesn't know how to fix it. It probably would have been stupid for me to tell her to get Dad to come home. That would fix me.

I know I have to be careful about the emotions coming out in front of the kids, and then again, maybe not. I don't want to shake their world anymore than it already has been, but letting them see me cry hopefully makes them know that it is all out there in the open and they can show their emotions openly too. At least I hope so. I hope they will all grant me a break and let me cry. It's what I do best now. It's all I know.

As my life has taken this new, drastic turn, I am left to navigate all the things I should be doing, or all the things I think I should be doing and all the things I don't want to do. In truth, I really don't want to do anything. I don't want to make changes and more than anything I just don't want to acknowledge these changes. I just don't. This becomes a constant struggle for me as I try to go through my day to day while not acknowledging that everything has changed. Some of the most intangible issues I struggle with are just in the simple handling of the question, "How are you?" I suck!! I scream it in my head, but the best I can do is to simply say, "I'm hanging in there." It's the only truth I know. That, and pain of course. That is all I can muster is to simply hang in and hang on. By a thread, only by a thread.

Eight

"Anymore," a word that haunts me yet stays constant in my head, like a skipping record. Not anymore, not anymore, not anymore. My life, not anymore. My love, not anymore. My dreams, not anymore. My hopes, not anymore. My future, not anymore. My constant companion, not anymore.

I wonder if I say it and write it over and over if I will process it any better. Grief, my constant companion. Grief, my future. Grief, my life. I am so empty that I don't know where I will get the strength to fight through this pain with its vapid loneliness for one more day. Really, another day? How about another hour? The pain today is that much. The pain is overwhelming and over-powering and I'm afraid that it is winning. My stomach is in knots. I don't know what that means because I don't remember having this too much when Wes was sick. I feel like I'm drowning and my stomach is telling me so. Your body tells you the things you need to know. Someone throw me a life preserver because I'm going under. Wes is the only life preserver that will help me, and he's not here. Not anymore.

I have to go into work after having a total meltdown. These primal cries are scaring me. They come from so down deep that I don't know what to do with them, except let them flow. And that they do until I'm depleted. Like an athlete that gives all that they have until they are totally depleted and spent. Only I'm not an athlete anymore. In fact, I'm afraid I am just a shell of my former self. I don't think I have anything left to even deplete. What a day I'm having. I can't wait to see what tomorrow brings.

But I feel so unsettled. I don't feel good anywhere. Not here. Not at the beach. Nowhere. I'm constantly thinking, Where do I go and what do I do? How do I escape this? The pain, the grief and the worry are exacerbating the damage to my heart and soul. The decisions I have to make are truly overwhelming, with houses to take care of, work, three kids…that are actually taking care of me, two dogs, one, not my own, my father, estates to settle, washing machines to replace, leaks in hot water lines, front porch railings that need to be replaced. These collective responsibilities are drowning me. It's all too much and I don't know what to do. My future looks like a huge void. In fact, there is nothing in my head and psyche about my future except for this huge black void. I guess that's what sadness looks like.

I can't stop crying today. I've been sobbing for the last three days. We are back to primal cries and sobs. My stomach hurts and I think I'm going to throw up. I'm pretty sure I am. I am supposed to leave right now to go and meet Mark for estate stuff and I am sitting here in sweats and a sweatshirt with tears running down my nose and face. I don't think you would like it if you saw me right now Wesley. I'm in a bad way. Not a pleasing sight, but I am too weak to do anything else. I want to call Mark and tell him I can't make it. I feel like a baby for this but I just can't do it. So I call Mark and cry. I know it's not fair to do this to other people but I am just too weak to manage anything else right now. I simply have no energy for anything. Four months today, it already feels like it's been years. Not only do I feel like I weigh a thousand pounds again, but I also have this crushing pain in my chest that tells me that I'm suffocating. Grief weighs a ton and then it smushes you.

The sobs seem to have left me for the moment. Maybe I should have tried to get to Mark's office but the thought of sitting there trying to absorb what is going on would have been a bust. I am ready to short circuit. No more info, no more pain, no more grief, no more broken appliances; I am overloaded. Wes come home, the washing machine is broken.

The reality is that I just want to go to sleep and wake up a year from now. It probably won't happen, but I could use a break from this hurt. I remember the raw pain when my mother died when I was just nineteen. I learned what the finality of death really means when she died. There's no going back, no turning the clock back for one more hour, one more minute, one more second. Once that window is shut, there is no opening it again. This pain of losing Wes is excruciating and I'm drawn to all the pictures of him. I am trying to get into the pictures, to feel him and to touch him. I sob, then I smile, but mostly I just yearn. I still think I will see him again. I remember that feeling from my mother's death as well. But I haven't seen her yet and it's been a really long time. I struggle to reconcile the length of time until I will see him again. He was so full of life and all the pictures of him tell the same story. I get lost in the photos and in the memories of the moments each one was taken and then I get a shot of reality and I am taken aback by the momentum of the grief that slams into me again and again and again. I can't get away from it. It comes at me like the waves in a storm as they continuously batter me into the surf and into submission. I just wish the waves would take me once and for all. I don't have the energy to fight this fight. The undertow is winning and it's taking me under and it's taken me to the depths of the ocean floor as I get slammed into the sand and tossed around like a rag doll as I continuously get pummeled by the pain and grief of losing my bestie, my lover and my soulmate. I simply can't get my footing to push myself through the ferocious waves and right myself in the direction of the sunlight. Push Sharon. Kick your feet. Swim. Fight, just fight, for one more minute. I can't. And I don't want to. Take me now God, I'm already half dead anyway.

But God doesn't listen to me this time either. I'm really beginning to hate this guy. He is the constant in my thoughts as well, as I fully and totally hold Him responsible for Wes' death. Of course He didn't listen to me. He never does. Ever. As I struggle through this day, I listen to Wes' voicemail again. I haven't cut his phone off and I don't know if I will. I listen to his voice and I just sink. I get surf pummeled again. I loved his voice. It just rang so melodic in my ears. It was the reassurance in the day that I grew so accustomed to and relied on so heavily. The voice…Wes' voice. It is the constant in my day. Or it was. But not anymore. And as I struggle to reconcile how we've made it four months without him, I can't figure out how I have gotten this far. This far in a road that may never end for me, but I missed him even when he went to work or away for a trip. We were all drawn to Wes. I just liked being with him and around him. As we all did. I miss the magic of Wesley. It is so hard to not have that magnet around anymore. There's that word again: anymore. Not anymore. My life as I know it, not anymore.

Grief is turning into a scattered emotion and response. These thoughts that pop into my head constantly are written down on these pages quickly so I can capture the emotion and I can understand it, at its most raw and undefined moment. Welcome to my world, it's Hell in here. But I sometimes think that if I just block out the pain, and force myself to move forward, it will be better. Maybe I can survive this brutality by avoiding it all together. But I know better. I know that I have to deal with this head on because if I don't, it will assuredly come back to haunt me somewhere down the line. In theory, suppressing the grief sounds great, but the truth is I don't have an ounce of strength to suppress anything. It would take so much mental and emotional energy to try to suppress what I am feeling and I just don't have it to give. I certainly have no extra energy to spare. My tire is flat.

I am exhausted today. Three days of intense crying has worn me out. I'm tired just thinking about what is on my to-do list today. I end up working and I am productive. That is a big deal for me. In my current situation, that is. It is now 10:20 p.m. and in thirty minutes it will have been four months exactly since Wes passed. I hate this day. I hate four months and I hate missing Wes. I knew more love by being with him and as I now know more pain by being without him. How will I carry on what he started? His love, his laughter, his outlook, his promise? How? I'm not equipped to be Wes. That's just a fact. He was always my example of goodness as I constantly tried to be a better person because of him. Now what? Now, bloody hell, what? I need the Wes structure, the Wes guidance and the Wes example. I'm a slow learner. I need Wes to be my example for at least the next thirty years. He needs to show me the way. I will fail without him. Come home Wes and save me, from myself.

My night doesn't end much better. I had a bad dream last night and it was disturbing. It really shook me up. I dreamt Wes was getting sick outside of our car before he passed. I was getting him out of the car and he was so weak and he knew it was the end for him and he got sick. That did not happen in real life but this dream was so vivid and I couldn't sleep even with the Ambien I was taking. I am worried over what my day will bring in terms of emotional distress. I've had a hell of a week and I don't know how much more I can take of this crying at this heightened intensity. I am going to head to the beach but still can't get myself calm. Calm enough to get there or calm enough to even just exist, even for the moment. I am not eating again. I don't even think about it until 2:00 p.m. today and then I only had cold Chipotle. I see Wes' picture on the kitchen counter and his smile melts my heart, and then my heart breaks all over again and now the tears come. I didn't even get out the door and I'm on the floor crying. These pictures of Wes are killing me. More crying. Again. Or still, I've lost track. I may vomit. But I just end up screaming.

The crying gets me again, but this time I drag my friend Carol into it. She calls to check in on me and she gets an earful. I'm going through friends like you can't even believe. If you call to check in and ask me how I'm doing, be prepared for what may happen. And so it did. It happened again, more tears and I just let loose with Carol on the other end crying with me. I love someone who can cry with you and with intensity. Carol is my bestie in this. She willingly calls and willingly cries with me. I am curiously aware of all of this even in my worst moments and I am more grateful than I even have words to say. As this week keeps heaping on the distress, it has been brutal for me. Brutal on my heart and brutal on my friends.

Carol's sister Jane lost her husband suddenly a year before Wes died. Jane calls me too. She has been awesome and probably the one person through all of this that keeps me going in terms of how much can I really take. Trudging through this pain. She becomes my gauge of tolerance. She keeps telling me it will get better and that you don't love them any less or miss them any less, you just navigate differently. I want to run as far away from this pain as I can. Run away from this plan and run from this new navigation process I am supposed to inhabit, but I sense it will find me. It always does.

I get invitations to do things, genuine invitations that are amazing, but I can't do them. I just can't do them. Almost none of them in fact. The peanut butter has me cemented in one place. I can't muster talking with anyone, or seeing anyone, let alone doing anything. I'm in a really bad place. Really bad. I'm scaring myself. My sister invites me to a spa day and as nice as the thought is, all I feel immediately upon hearing the suggestion is that my whole person is being suffocated and drowned. I can't even fathom the idea of sitting in one place for more than five minutes. That five minute rule applies to more than just the food on a dirty floor, as it applies to those that are grieving and cannot get themselves out of their own way.

I am like a caged animal that is feeling its fate is challenged and the outcome is unsure. Everything is coming down on me right now, I am at the pinnacle of this grief cycle and I am headed down a bad trajectory that is taking me straight into the depths of grief hell. I can't go to a spa, I can't talk to anyone and I can't be confined to any one area. When I decline, my sister texts me back and says, "You know you are isolating don't you?" I want to scream and say f – off!! What do you know anyway? But I text back politely and say, "Who cares?" I can't be analyzed, unless I'm paying for it. It dawns on me that I need to make an appointment to be analyzed because I am cracking up. I am going over a cliff and it is happening faster than I have brakes to stop it or even the energy to press down on the pedal. I am in a hateful place. I only want to be with the kids right now. Not because I want to anchor myself to them, because I at least know they have a right to live their life, but I want to be with them because I don't want to have to explain myself to anyone. With them I don't have to and there can actually be some levity sometimes in our conversations because we are at the same place. We don't have to explain it because we know it already.

As I write in this journal and bare the depth of this pain that curses me as it courses through my veins, I'm not even sure what its purpose is, if there even is one. Maybe it will eventually show the evolution of pain. Raw, abject pain transforming into something more manageable? I don't know if that will happen. After the week I've been having I can't even imagine it. I'm in it deep. Really deep and right now I am exposed pain like an exposed nerve with air being blown on it. When that happens at the dentist it is pure torture. Navigating this pain makes going to the dentist seem like a vacation.

Jane keeps telling me that we have to go on for our kids because they need us. Really? I think I need them. I think they are keeping me up, holding me up and keeping my head above the water that I want to go under so badly. But they keep buoying me up. I have used the line endlessly with Sean in his high school years that you can't buoy someone else up when you are drowning yourself. Now as I think about it, I think I may be a boundary issue for my kids. Good God, don't let me be the burden, their burden. But as Jane continues to tell me that Wes and Mike would want us to go on and take care of the kids and they are pushing us to stay strong. Right now, this week, today, I only half believe her. But earlier Carol told me that Jane was crying and saying it was all bullshit because she knew that Mike wanted to be here with her and the girls. What I know for a fact is that God has this wrong. We still had lessons to learn from Wes and Mike. We need them here.

Nine

I think about Wes during the time he was in the hospital before he passed away, and I remember a day when I came into the room and he was really upset. I asked him what was wrong, which seemed like a very silly question under the circumstances. He could have easily said, "Everything Sharon, pretty much everything." But he didn't. That wasn't Wes' way. What he did tell me was how scared he was and how he was worried about how much he was going to miss the kids and me. I wish I had those moments back. I don't know that I would have had any better or more comforting words for him, but I was fighting the emotion to call it, "game over." And so I didn't. I still couldn't bring myself to throw in the towel. Wessy, I will never give up on you, ever. In retrospect, I may have caused him more angst by not letting go and not giving into the cancer. Surely, he had given in to his reality, but I couldn't. But maybe he just wanted to talk. Maybe he wanted to tell me a few more things. Maybe he wanted to tell me to move on, and not hang on. Maybe he wanted to let me know how to move forward. What I would give for those moments again. I'd suck it up. I'd suck up my fear and my stubbornness of not giving in and I'd just listen. I'd listen to his beautiful voice tell me everything he wanted to tell me. Everything he wanted me to tell the kids. Maybe everything about life that I needed to know that night and at that moment and that would last me a lifetime. Maybe he would tell all that I needed to know. Maybe he just needed me to just listen. But I didn't. I just couldn't. Again, it just felt like such a betrayal to agree that he wasn't going to make it. The year of magical thinking was actually existent even leading up to his death. I just couldn't reconcile the process, and so I didn't, which is another thing that beats me up as time goes by.

Each day seems like a landmark day. First week, first month, first holiday, first anniversary, there is always something lingering atop the trees waiting to be lauded as the first of something. It's always looming there in this first year of grief. I guess in a mental capacity, these "firsts" help us garner strength for the next first that shows up uninvited. But what I do know is that they are ever present and therefore something that the bereaved are always conscious of and anticipate with almost an eerie vengeance. It may very well be that these firsts end up being the connection we have to our loved one, and on some insane level it's all we can focus on. No chance of balancing your chakras, when your bestie grief is at your beck and call.

In our huge king sized bed, I am alone. I wake up and find that I've slept on Wes' side of the bed for part of the night. I'm restless at night now, even on Ambien, and it makes for tough days. Tougher, that is. I wake up wrapped up in Wes' t-shirts and I start to try to relive our life together. Grief is a mind game. It's all about keeping things as they were and are, and staying in the past. Cement yourself in the past. Don't move and don't give in to this new reality. The problem is, the future keeps coming at you.

I fall asleep crying and I wake up doing the same. I'm not in Wes' strong arms, but instead wrapped up again in his t-shirts that are my lifeline. I'm crying and begging him to come home. Games we play with ourselves. I figured for sure he was listening. Sundays were our favorite. It always included coffee, bagels, and a drive first thing in the morning. It was just our thing. We front loaded date night for first thing in the morning. I wake up and don't have a clue what to do. Now what? What am I supposed to do today? I've got nothing and I'm spent. A night of crying and waking up crying has worn me out. I've had a couple of weeks of feeling stronger and now the onslaught is happening again. The grief rollercoaster. I'm feeling like I did the first few weeks after Wes died. It's hitting me that hard again.

This time, though, my anger is coming out. I am so angry at Wes for leaving me. It is so absurd to feel this anger, under the circumstances, but it too is part of grief. I'm looking at his pictures and giving him the what for right to his face. In his face – you better believe it. Mark tells me I have to go to the DMV and tell them Wes is gone. I need to tell them to take him out of their system. He is no longer here. I need to show them the death certificate, which angers me more than anything. I hate those notices, notarized, no less, to make them authentic and legal. My husband is not here anymore, that's pretty fucking authentic. How's that for authentic? The process is grim, and I reject it with everything in me. Don't you dare make me tell you he is gone. Don't make me stand in line at the DMV and hand you his notice. The problem with these formalities and the experience at the DMV is that it almost trivializes your person. My person being Wes. It makes it just a computer adjustment, when in real life it is traumatizing. One more separation. And of all places, taking your most sacred to the most banal, cold, unfriendly, and hateful places. It makes me cry just thinking about it. I hate going there to renew a license, but now I'm supposed to tell them Wes is gone and I've got the documents to prove it. Screw them, screw the DMV and screw everybody. Whoever said that, "Life sucks and then you die," is an idiot. Anger is a tough beast. I should know, I'm living with it.

But my anger is really ratcheting up. I am mad at Wes for leaving me and I am mad at everyone for having a life. It is so surreal to listen to friends taking great trips and stressing over flights and arrangements. Try taking this flight I've been on for the last five months. Now that's something to stress about. I can't wrap my head around how life continues on around me and mine has essentially stopped. I'm mad. I'm really mad about that. And I'm mad at everyone who doesn't know how mad I am.

Disbelief gets harder and harder every day. As I still can't believe that Wes isn't here anymore. I can't believe I'm a widow. I think Wesley, I should be your wife for another twenty years at least. You promised me fifty years together and more if we got lucky. You owe me more time. You promised me when you married me, when I was only twenty-three and walking down the aisle, scared to death, you promised. This was our promise of our lifetime. We had the whole package. Wessy come home, you owe me more time.

Kara calls me and she is crying. Life is painful and confusing and she is trying to muddle through and make sense of things. She is feeling Wes' absence and the safety of a father as she struggles to navigate all things in this living world. It makes me cry to hear her and to understand the depth of a daughter losing the compass and the security of her father. I get it, I certainly do. It is revealed that she isn't sure what she wants to do with her life and she feels obligated to me. Of course they do. I get that as well. I felt the same way when my mother died and I had the same feelings of obligation to and for my father. Feeling tethered is tough to navigate. Understanding that, I tell Kara specifically that I am untethering her and that she needs to move on. Taking care of me is going to have to start being my job. Sean and I had almost this identical conversation, I told him the same thing. He said Wes told him that he needed to man up and be there to help take care of the family. I told him that dad would never hold him back from moving on and moving forward. I guess the time is here that I have to understand what being on my own is really like. I'm going to hate every minute of it, but I know it is coming. I know it is, because I also realize that Jake will be leaving to go back to school after withdrawing after Wes died. He too, needs to move on, and I can tell he is ready to head back to school. It is gratifying to know that all of my three children are working towards the future and what it will hold for them. Conversely, I am working towards the past because it was the happiest time of my life. How do we move forward and through and try to get through the tunnel when we are clearly trying to achieve different objectives? Life is tough and then you get sucker punched.

I often think about how Wes would have handled this if it were me that had died. I think he would have done much better. For one, his friends wouldn't have let him spend a moment alone, and Wes was really good at reaching out. He had no problem letting someone know he didn't want to be alone. I struggle with all of that. And as a result I end up waiting for a phone call or holing up because I don't know what else to do.

The fourth of July is here and we are at the beach. Kara heads down to the beach and once I'm alone, I lose it with a force that scares me. I cry at the top of my lungs and I scream and pace and fall on the floor. I'm a caged animal again. I want the pain to stop. I cannot endure this pain. Truly, it is taking me over and will take me under. I am absolutely certain of it. I leave Wes a text message and I've listened to his voicemail twice in the last ten minutes. My heart is broken. I can't stand this. I cannot. Every ounce of me is weak. I have no reserves. I need him. I need Wes. I need him in person and not on his voicemail. I can't do this alone. For crying out loud, and I am, Wesley, come home.

Kara keeps calling me to come down to the beach. I literally have to pick myself up and move my feet to get there. And this process of moving my feet on this day, right now, is monumental. On top of this, Kara wants me to bring sandwiches down and oh yea, could you put some avocadoes on them? For the love of Pete. I can barely get my suit on. This request is like an out of body experience. Avocadoes? I'm on the floor crying. "I'll be there in a bit," I say. And I know I have to get down there too. I can't upset her and make her worry, more than she already does anyway. So I do. I move my feet and make sandwiches with avocado and make my way to the beach. By the time I get there, I am absolutely exhausted and depleted of all energy. I have nothing. I'm just spent.

I remember this day so clearly. I remember the sheer anguish I was experiencing alone in the house and the sheer determination to put on a face to go sit on the beach and join the living and breathing. I remember sitting there in a chair under an umbrella and our friend Tom coming over and sitting down in the chair next to me. He was trying to chat and all I could muster were the simplest of answers, and nothing else. There was this separate part of me acting as the spectator feeling horrible that I couldn't engage more, but at the same time, thinking Tom, you don't know this but I have literally been crawling on my hands and knees at the house and screaming and hurling at the top of my lungs. I've got nothing to give here. I know he is concerned, after all it had only been five months since Wes passed, and everyone is feeling it. These pains aren't exclusive to me, but I haven't heard stories of the others clawing around on the carpet trying to get air. Maybe they all have better ways of dealing with this. I find comfort in the lioness that has taken up residence inside my body. Foreign as it might be, it too is becoming my bestie because it is quickly becoming all that I know.

We rely on so many people to help us get through, and I cherish the love and support that the kids and I have received from everyone. All of our friends and family and all of the Goons. Wes' friends are always here for us and as I look to them to see Wes, I know they are doing the same. We need each other. Plain and simple.

So many times, people will mention to me how much they miss Wes, and I say, "I know, I do too," and then the tears well up. It worries people and upsets them when they think they have upset me. I tell them, I do this all day long, they didn't do it and I love that they are talking about Wes. He's my favorite subject, so I want people to keep talking about him, to keep telling me stories, because it makes him still alive to all of us and that is the best thing. It is healing in an abstract way, even with the tears. But I couldn't bear for anyone to not tell me a Wes story just because I might cry. Keep the stories coming. They make me feel that Wes is close. Those stories are a gift in this dark nightmare.

When I hit the five-month mark since Wes died, it felt like years. When I include the time spent while he was sick, it feels like a decade. My grief counselor tells me five months is a tough one. Maybe some of the shock is wearing off and all I we've got is the reality. It sits heavy on me, like an elephant.

Six months pass. I've survived six months and I can't believe it. And I did two big things this week. I made an appointment for my hair to be cut and highlighted and I made a dentist appointment. The hair appointment was a gift certificate from Wes and the kids for my fiftieth birthday. Obviously, Wes was sick and I didn't get a chance to go, nor did I want to. After Wes died, I had even less of a desire to go. The fear of sitting there crying with tin foil wrapped all over my head was worrying me, crushing me actually. Small talk is out of the question, so the appointment was never set up until now. The certificate had written on it from, "Wes and the Kids." It is probably the last thing Wes gave me, except for his heart and soul. As I was getting ready to leave and was walking out of my room I started crying. I had a tightening in my chest again and rapid breathing. I felt like I was suffocating. Why did I think I could do this? I couldn't even get out of my bedroom. I tried to get a grip but the tears came and started rolling down my cheeks again and in a free fall on my lap. I called my sister and she didn't answer. I called Laurie and she didn't answer, and I called Nancy and she answered and I started sobbing just hearing her say hello. I told her what was going on and she understood and just walked me through it. So many times she and Laurie have walked me through it while holding my hand over the phone. A gift. I got to the salon feeling stronger. When my hair was being cut I caught a glimpse of myself in the mirror. Man, do I look old.

Ten

Taking care of Wes' phone is like a full time job. Making sure that it doesn't get low on battery, I am constantly plugging it in to recharge it. The phone, as a symbol, is the only living thing I have of Wes. It speaks to me after all. His voice, telling me he can't come to the phone, "but leave a message and I'll get back to you as soon as I can. Thank you very much." His voice: strong, steady and melodic to my ears. It is so alive that I want to grab him. He has to be here, right? His voice is so strong, it's so present, it's what I've listened to a million times. Where are you Wes, I can hear you but I can't find you. Deluded games preside over the mind and I can see that it could be easy to get stuck here. Delusions almost seem safer.

There are four pillows on the bed and now the bed houses a couple of Wes' t-shirts that I now hold and wrap around my neck when I'm sleeping. My sleep patterns are different. I have slept wound so tight when Wes got sick that I would wake and my chest had a persistent ache, my shoulders hurt, as did my jaw. I was so stressed during his illness that I never relaxed, ever. Every night I would clench my fists and hold onto myself, when not holding onto him, with everything I had in me and I would sleep like that until the day he died. The occurring chest pain I was certain was some kind of heart attack or the prelude to. I have been waking up with pain in my hamstrings and shoulders and chest. I am tense. I sleep tense. I feel like I've had the work out of a lifetime when I wake up in the morning. I find myself rolled into the smallest ball I can get into, like a roly poly bug that curls up when they feel threatened. My shoulders ache, as do my elbows, all from holding myself so rigid and tight from the stress. I curl up as tight as I can so the world won't catch up to me. I try to stretch out while I'm sleeping and even when awaking, but just like a rubber band, I go right back into a ball. Only with a hot flash can I straighten myself out and stay there. But only until the flash passes, then I instinctively wind back up into protective mode. I think I'm the size of a nickel. I want this pain to go away and for Wes to come and make me feel safe again. But he doesn't, and all I end up with is a Charlie horse.

As I come out of the bathroom I see the pillows on Wes' side of the bed under the covers. His t-shirts were there and I fooled myself for a split second thinking he was there. He's not Sharon. You are alone. As I go to make the bed, I walk around to Wes' side and I end up lying down on his side of the bed crying. God I miss you.

I'm thinking of his hands again. They keep coming into my mind. How can I not have his hand to hold? I need to feel his strength by feeling the safety in his grip. Safety, the key word. Isn't it crazy that his hands held so much security for me? Now, all I have is a couple of t-shirts.

I told Nancy I wasn't coming over tonight. Well, actually I texted her. The chicken way, but I wasn't up for the discussion. True to form, she kept calling me on my home phone and on my cell. She was leaving me messages to pick up the phone and not to ignore her. Truly, I was, but for the love of Pete, she wasn't having any part of it. So I picked up the phone and just told her I was in a bad place. I'm actually becoming aware of being a downer for people, so I resist. That isn't easy to deal with either. She told me that's what they're here for. Anyway, we kept it as is, and I will hang low tonight. Now that I've gotten some of the crying out, I'm ready to go to her house, but now I'm uninvited. Criminy.

I get into bed in the middle of the day. I don't allow myself to do that too often, because I'm astute enough to know it could be an emotional trap. But today, I have no choice. I get back in my bed and sob. Primal cries that actually scare Jake's dog, Mia. She sits by my bed whining, but I have no energy to make it better for her, as I have no energy to make it better for myself. I sleep for a bit and then doze some more. I have dreams of Wes that wake me up in tears. I remember the times that I would sneak up to lay on my bed to read in the afternoon, on the rare days that I actually could pull it off, and I would invariably doze off. Wes would come up and I'd hear him put his hat on the chest at the end of our bed, slip off his shoes and he would come in and spoon me. I would be on my side so there wasn't a ton of room between me, and the edge of the bed, but he would slip in and hold me and we'd nap for a little while. Sweet memories. I was hoping for that today but Wes didn't show in real time. But as I dozed off, I had a very real moment and a very real sense that he was there. In my dream, I heard him step down the little step into our room. I heard the bill of his baseball cap hit the wood on the chest at the end of our bed. I felt the bed sink slightly from the weight of his hand as he held onto it while slipping off his shoes. I felt all of it. I felt him next to me. To this day, I feel the intensity of that nap and that experience. I know Wes was around me.

I remember when Wes was first diagnosed. I was in our bathroom with my IPod on, playing Van Morrison's "These are the Days." As Wes walked in, he and I instinctively reached for each other and started slow dancing right there, in front of the vanity, holding onto each other for dear life and crying. Those moments between two people are the soul of a relationship. Wes and I needed each other more than we ever had, but never needed to say anything at that moment because everything we felt was the same for the other. A connection between two people that are facing some of the toughest parts of what life dishes out and yet, even at the worst, what we needed, was each other. Van Morrison has always been one of my favorites. Now it just hurts to hear his songs and melodies, so I can't listen to him anymore. I want to slow dance with Wes again, but because we love each other, not because we are afraid. That day is etched in my mind as one with just raw, abject pain. My sweet Wesley, I hurt so much for you on that day and every day since.

I am having a moment again and I can't breathe. Oh please don't go into the closet and find his clothes. But I am having a closet moment again, except I'm not actually in the closet this time. This time I'm rolling around on my bedroom floor. Through my insanity, I am able to step outside myself and act as a spectator to the lunacy as I roll around on the carpet, moaning these deep, deep crazed and primal cries. It's just more of the same. I've been here before. I keep asking Wes to save me. I'm not asking, I'm begging and screaming. Please come and take care of me Wesley, I'm dying inside, same as you, but from a broken heart. My body is shutting down. My chest is tightening, the sobs are more intense and my resolve is gone.

Grief is a crazy animal. You can be despondent in your grief, but still have the other side of your brain keep a stopwatch that somehow keeps prodding you along saying, "You have to go to work. Better wrap this little grief session up and get moving." As I roll around on the floor, my work phone is ringing in my office downstairs. That pseudo silent voice in my head that keeps nudging me to get to work has now changed to a ringing reminder. Like an alarm clock.

I think about all the times I've been locked in our closet, with the doors that actually have no locks, or the times I'm rolling around on my floor, anywhere actually, because I've rolled around on every ounce and piece of real estate I own. Rolling, screaming, moaning, sobbing and just plain writhing on the floor. Even at my worst, I am vaguely, or astutely aware of what lunacy lurks beneath my skin and resides in my heart and head. But I can't help it, I have nowhere to let it loose but in these spaces and if it hurts this much to let this pain out, I can only imagine how much it would hurt if I tried to hold it in. This pain is a beast, and I can't fathom how much worse off I'd be if I tried to suppress it all. I'm pretty sure I would combust. There are no walls big enough or strong enough to hold this pain. Letting 'er rip is all I've got. And so I do.

But I can still be a spectator to my own lunacy, and yet not have a way to conceal it, control it, or even make it subside. I've realized from the beginning that allowing myself to feel every bit of this pain and grief is the only thing that will save me. Somehow I am smart enough to know that, and at the very least I know this inherently. Even in my worst moments, even when I didn't care what happened to me, even when I wasn't sure if I would make it out of the closet or even get up off the floor, I still knew I had to let the pain come. And so it has, and as I walk through this I go from five months to six months and I break down my loss in terms of days, and hours and even minutes. That's how I maneuver, that's how I make it from month five to month six.

When I am deep into the pain (more so the active pain, the crying and the yelling) I seem to be able to watch myself from afar, more of the spectator again. Even at my worst times, my conscious self might think I'm crazy, or at least in the process of going mad, but it also feels pain. Is that crazy, and does it sound crazy? Probably, and maybe, but I can stand outside of myself and witness what I'm going through and it hurts the part of me that is sane and that part that is connected. Maybe that's my subconscious watching out for the pained part of me, and maybe that's the way it works anyway. But in my sane mind, if there is one, I'm really not bragging, maybe it's my grounded mind, I know that part of me has to be lifting me up someway and somehow. But even at my worst times, I stand outside of myself and even I get scared. Maybe that's not saying much, because I feel like I've been scared for what feels like a lifetime now.

I go to Michelle, my grief counselor today, and she gave me so much to think about. I will have to wait to think about it all because now I can't remember any of it or anything that she said. I am overloaded. It will come back to me slowly, because that will be how I have to process it all, but I have shut it all down, nothing else can penetrate this head and heart of mine. It's broken, plain and simple.

But as the days go on, I do start remembering all the connections that were made in my grief session. It's tough, but all the sentiments of family and friends swirl around my head with nothing to grasp onto. I try to hold onto things that are said, but invariably, they don't stick. I try to assimilate, but they won't stay. There's a disconnect between my brain and my ability to verbalize. My brain just doesn't work. It is almost like it has been shut off. I cannot hold onto a thought and then I also can't articulate. The words just won't come.

During this time, the rawest point in all of my grief, it is astonishing that I ever came out of the closet, or stopped rolling around on my bedroom floor. These moments are too many to categorize, but fresh in my head as I wonder how in the world I was able to keep walking, keep trying, or even just keep breathing. As I think about all of those times, the million times actually, that I was immobilized by the pain of losing Wes, I am also amazed that I actually got up from any one of those moments. Losing Wes has been the singular most devastating event in my life. I've had a few of those moments, but losing Wes was like losing my outer skin. My protection, my shield, the love of my life, and of course, my joy. Life ain't easy, then you get thrown in with the dirty clothes.

As I hit the six month mark, this too feels like a lifetime. I can't believe I haven't seen Wes for six months. How can that be possible? I wake up and can't get out of bed because I don't have a clear direction for the day. That scares me, especially today. This feels like a milestone of the worst kind. I have a tightening in my chest this morning and my stomach hurts and I'm full of dread. This anniversary is part of my problem. I'm afraid of the loneliness. I'm afraid of what it will do to me. The loneliness is killing me and it will kill me, it will have to.

I'm not strong enough for this pain. I get up and I run some errands and I call Wes' phone and I start bawling. I leave a message but am sobbing and I beg him to answer and to come home. Wesley, just come home and let me hold you. My usual. My messages don't change.

This six month mark isn't just about bringing in an anniversary, it also heralds the inevitable departure of Jake for Radford. I realize I only have two more weeks before he leaves. I'm going to miss him so much. I love watching him walk in the door. That big smile, dimples, and big, enormous blue eyes that make me smile. It's been great having him home here, although he had to withdrawal from school. But I think it has been best, that the four of us have been here trying to get through this together. Maybe it is the only way. None of this has been easy for him. He left for Radford with Wes being sick, and he had to come home to say goodbye to him. As he tried to go back to school and sit through classes, it proved to be too tough. I get it. I've been there. My mom died at the same age as Wes and I was the same age as Jake. I too, tried to go back to school. I didn't work. But I have to help Jake get there and be productive. He's been home with all of us these last six months, while working full time and we've been getting through it together. I know there is fear for several reasons, but I can tell he's ready. He's ready to start his life, really start it this time. But it is also my job now to send him off with him feeling confident that it will be okay. I love you Jake, go to school and reach for the stars.

I get a reprieve this Sunday morning, as they tend to be some of the hardest parts of the week. Sunday mornings especially were Wes' and my time. But Sean comes in from a night out in Arlington with all of his friends. They had a blast, I could tell. I believe with all certainty that there was a lot of drinking going on. He came in looking like he had had a long night but he told me stories and I laughed as hard as I would have if Wes were telling me stories about the Goons. The legacy lives on and I'm not surprised, but I was more surprised at my ability to laugh. It felt good. Thank you Sean, for the stories. I'm still laughing.

I get an email from Greek this morning. Well, I see it in the morning, Greek sent it at 2:00 a.m. There may have been wine involved. But it was a sweet note telling me that I was strong and that I had to move on and not feel like I am leaving Wes behind. Which is exactly what I feel like. Moving forward seems so disloyal and I don't want to be disloyal to Wes, ever. But Greek is right, of course. I can't keep this up, the depression, the anxiety and the grief. It's just too hard and although I know I have to find my way, I have no idea how. I mean really, how?

Eleven

I dreamt of Wes last night. He came to me, I feel it in my bones. This type of dream is called a visitation dream. I know this because I looked it up. Our loved ones come to us in our dreams to let us know they are okay, and probably to try to take care of us. Wes always took care of me. The dream had a crazy setting, and we were in a group hotel room or house, with two double beds and Greek was in one bed and Wes and I were in the other. I was getting ready to hold Wes and he rolled on his back so that he could hold me, and he had me under his arm and he was kissing my head. This dream seemed so real to me and I could feel every part of his body while I rested in his arms. The way his hands felt touching me, and me holding his hand; strong and secure and safe. The yearning for the physical Wes never leaves me and never lessens. I could smell him, his familiar masculine, wonderful Wes smell. They are embedded in my senses for life. They will always be in my senses. I woke up this morning so grateful for the dream. Grateful that he came to me and let me know he was there. He was strong, calm and in control and therefore, so was I. I always am whenever he is around, whether in real life or in my reality now, which consists of dreams. But they comfort me, and this one in particular. I can feel him around me with his arms holding me and I am safe. I feel the softness of his lips, gently kissing my forehead and I am thankful. In real life, this was a beautiful feeling, in my dreams, it's my beautiful existence. Please Wes, don't ever leave me, please keep visiting me in my dreams. This is your reality now, Sharon, dreams of Wes. And so it is.

It's been a productive morning. I found a few pictures of Wes from his Babe Ruth days and Little League Football. I was cleaning out some drawers and found the team pictures. He was handsome, even then, at nine, twelve and fourteen. I found some of his business cards as well. It hits me hard, but I take a stack and throw out the rest. This little exercise is huge for me. I am purging, or at least trying. But I still can't touch his clothes and I don't want to. I don't want to be alone, but I am. I don't want to face the empty side of his closet. I don't want to face it and I just simply can't. I can't bear it. And so I don't. His clothes stay.

Jake said to me yesterday, "Mom, I had all of Dad's clothes on last night." I loved every bit of it and I told him so. I wash the clothes he wears of Wes' and return them back to Wes' side of the closet. Jake notices that. I told him that I like it when he comes and gets them. I guess it makes me feel like there is still life in my closet. The mind is tricky and it has to be appeased, no matter how insane it seems.

But Jake's last day of work is today, before he goes back to school. Every day gets closer to him leaving. I will miss him. Every day he comes home to take care of Mia, his dog, and therefore he is here and I've come to rely on that. He always checks in with me when he gets home, no matter what time it is. I've come to relish those connections. In this world, when life is short, the little gestures are huge and I am grateful.

Wes ignores me for the last two nights. He's a no-show in my dreams. I feel like he is dissing me, and it hurts. The lunacy of grief does not escape me, and yet I am defenseless in my ability to rise above it. I'm nuts. There, I said it. My words could never do my emotions justice. There just aren't any to describe this hell. But sometimes these dreams are a setback emotionally after one of these vivid dreams, and actually, a lot of times it is. I seem to be on a high for a day after one of them, but then I can hardly wait to get back into bed and fall asleep so we can be together. It's usually my plan, and when Wes doesn't show, I get knocked down. I wake up and realize he didn't visit me and I am sad. I am lonely, I am alone and yet I am realizing this is my new normal. I wake trying to overcome this inherent sadness, putting schedules and pseudo-lists in my head in order to get through the day, or in reality, to actually get out of bed. This is new. Am I transitioning? Am I moving forward?

I get out of bed, not wanting to, but not wanting to stay either. I am motivated just in motions but not in mind. I am downstairs doing mindless tasks. Now I am back upstairs in my room getting changed to go on a bike ride. I need to get the heck out of here. I'm hurting a lot this morning and I need to get physical. I'm sad all over. I am in pain again. Physical pain. It is shooting through my chest like a piercing arrow. I might take an aspirin. Am I having a heart attack or is this anxiety? Who the hell knows, they both are crippling. Push yourself Sharon, push, push. Change and get on the bike, Abba and Dancing Queen are waiting for you on your IPod.

I ended up crying for a good portion of my bike ride. It was a tough ride. I got home and was very upset and sat at the kitchen table and cried more. They're back. Primal cries, but maybe not as loud or as forceful as before. I am now gauging the intensity of the cries as a barometer for the healing or the pain. Whichever way I look at it, I know that at the end of each crying jag, I will still be alone. In the beginning I believed that I would see Wes again, now maybe I know better and that knowledge cuts like a knife. I hate that realization. I want to see him again, of course I do. I want our family intact again, of course I do. Don't tell me that I can't have that. But maybe I know the truth now. Sort of. I can only grasp this truth in halves and quarters. There are no wholes for me, not now and not yet.

When I get home from my ride, I know my day is going to be shot in many ways, and that these emotions are here to stay. I can play this out in a couple of ways. I can do it alone, or I can ask for help. I decide to ask for help. I call my next door neighbor and dear friend Sandy, and ask for help. In truth, I never need to ask for help from Sandy, she knows me too well. If I call, she knows something is up and asks me over for coffee. Come over for your counseling session and a cup of java.

Sandy loved Wes. She totally got his quirks, his humor, and his personality. She always got the biggest kick out of him and she cries with me often. I know the tears are real and heartfelt. She feels the loss as much as we do. She puts things in perspective for me on this particular morning as she has done throughout his illness and since he has passed. I've come to rely on Sandy. I need her insight, and so she gives it. I try to assimilate the words and wisdom she bestows on me at her kitchen island over coffee, but nothing sticks. I have no mind. But yet I try. I have no memory or point of reference. It is crazy what is going on in my head. It's called grief, and it feels like my mind is walking through peanut butter.

I actually know what's happening to me today. I'm trying to let go of Jake. One more thing to let go of, and it's killing me. He's leaving on Monday and Kara and I are driving him down. I know my tears are partially associated with him leaving. I will miss him. He deserves to go and should go, and he deserves to go without me making him feel any stress. I try hard to get my head around that so I can give him that gift. It will indeed be a gift, because this is going to be hard to see him go, very, very hard.

Wes visits me in my dreams three times this week. Maybe he knows that Jake's departure will be hard on me, so he is showing up. Sometimes for just a snippet, other times a little longer. In this longer one, we are both in our office. I tell him I am going to make him a nutrition shake. It seems that I am acknowledging he's sick, but he seems healthy and strong. I'm angry at him now for leaving me. It's a new emotion to tangle with. I consider that this too is why he is evident in my dreams this week. Wes never liked when I was angry with him. He was a peace guy. He always wanted to make things better and make me "un-mad." It usually wasn't hard. He could say one thing and I would laugh. That was his magic. I'd try to resist his humor and stay mad, but he won every time. I couldn't resist his smile and his hug and I tried for thirty years. Wes was my perfect partner. He was so astute in his ability to get me outside of myself so I didn't take myself so seriously. I am so grateful for the lesson he gave me and taught me. He loved me regardless and he taught me to be lighter in spirit and in spite of myself. Thank you for the lessons Wesley, I love you forever.

Our youngest is going off to college in the morning, Wes. Kara and I follow him down and get him set up. We went to Walmart and got the essentials and helped him set up his room and bathroom. It was fun to be with him. He walks us out to the car and I start crying. He holds me tight and keeps saying, "Momma." We say goodbye, and he seems happy to be back at school and ready to start again, start strong. We get home late in the evening and Kara and I laugh on the ride back that Jake actually allowed us to help him out. I came upstairs and made the very conscious decision not to open his bedroom door. I will face that obstacle tomorrow. Tonight I am just going to relish in the fact that Jake was happy and that Kara and Sean are both home tonight. I am thankful for that, indeed.

I slept pretty well, I think. But I had a dream of Wes as I was starting to wake up. I was telling someone in the dream that Wes and I really needed to spend more time with each other, because we'd just been going a mile a minute. But I caught myself, in the dream mode, that he wasn't here and the reality hit me in the dream. Maybe I was telling Wes we needed to spend more time together. I don't know what the dream means and I don't like it. Just be with me in my dreams Wes. Don't make me realize you are no longer here. I deal with that every minute of every waking hour – just give me this gift during sleep. At this point, it's all I've got.

My emotions are on the surface and I am working hard to keep them in check. This is a constant in my life, my new life that is. If I don't get sleep, then a component of my resolve will not be there and I will crumble. This whole walk that I am walking is a perpetual gauge on the crumble factor. When, where and if. It is crazy to think like this but it is all about making it through the day and how well you do it. There are days I don't do it at all, but the sun sets and then rises the next day and I am reminded again and again by the sun that I am just an element in this universe and that no, the universe is not crumbling just because I am.

It's almost diabolical to think that the world hasn't stopped because of our loss. The world is not rocking because of this, but we are, in our little corner of the world. It is hard to adjust to this realization as Kara, Sean, Jake and I quake in our boots every waking minute knowing that Wes is not here with us.

Another dream. But this dream was of a wedding we were going to. We went to North Carolina on a private plane. I was waiting for Wes to show up all night in the dream. He stayed on the fringes of my dream and never really showed. This sleeping thing is now becoming torture. Since these visitation dreams are the only time I get to share a moment with him, I am hopeful every night falling asleep. But now he isn't showing and I am truly distressed upon waking.

It's a crazy dream in its vividness, but I remember waiting with a beating heart for Wes to show up in it. We were at the reception with tons of people and yet Wes stayed on the other side of a wall or door and wouldn't come forward to me, while I was waiting for him to come into the room. I was like a schoolgirl waiting for the boy she has a crush on except this crush was close to suffocating me. Wes never revealed himself from behind the wall and I felt like I was dying inside not being able to see him. I think I remember feeling hurt, like he didn't want to see me. Dying inside was the resounding emotion from my dream. I am dying inside every day, I die a little bit more because of my dream.

I analyze these dreams and for this one I rationalize that Wes is pulling away from me and that this is part of the cycle of grief. Either Wes' work is coming to an end or that I am letting go. I scream in my dream and while awake, "Do not leave me Wes, in my dreams or in my thoughts." I cannot take anymore loss. Please Wesley, don't leave my dreams. I need you. Still and forever.

I wanted to dance close to you in this dream, but I woke up alone, abandoned and heartbroken. This actually becomes more torturous than almost imaginable. Dreams should be lala land and make believe, but these dreams, my dreams of Wes are crushing me. It feels like he is leaving me twice and leaving me all over again. I get crushing blows of this reality because this loss is what I live every waking hour and now it is forcing me to acknowledge my reality in my dreams. Can it get any worse? I realize that I am literally fighting in my sleep to hold onto Wes and not let him leave. It has become equally as hard a fight as fighting for Wes' life. I cannot let go. Ever.

I have cried a lot today. It's been seven months since Wes died. It may as well be seven years. Today it feels like it just happened. It is a cold and raining day so it doesn't help my mood, but the night was a fighting one. I had all my fighting gear on. I kept waking and my fists and my jaw were clenched. I was rolled up in a tight ball and I was so angry. I wonder how my life got like this. I feel like I'm having a heart attack again. My chest hurts, but I think its anxiety. I am internalizing everything and am struggling to cope. I feel so isolated today. I am angry, so angry. A new emotion with such verve. It's scaring me. Today is a new low.

As we hit the seven month anniversary, I felt Wes around me everywhere. I was at the beach on that particular weekend and I even felt a little happy. These opposing emotions are a constant drain in their need to be monitored and managed. But when you get a day where there is some happiness, you take it. I did a lot of work on the beach house, maintaining it by painting outside and general upkeep. I wanted to honor Wes, so over the next four days I accomplished what I had set out to do. Feeling Wes' presence along with a burning desire to honor all he gave to us was pushing me forward. I felt his presence all day and all weekend. I felt strong.

But as these opposing emotions are the only constant on my emotional train these days, I am managing the positive presence of Wes but also the emotional emptiness of the loss of him as well. It never ends. Up and down. Emotions running amok and a constant strain to manage them in their best and in their worst.

Twelve

I am remembering so many of Wes' nuances now, but with a cost. These memories are like a burning ache in my heart because all of Wes' traits were his and his alone. They comprised him and I miss every single one of them. Wes never got on my nerves, well okay, maybe we would get on each other's nerves, but not for his attributes, those I adored. His actions could exasperate me, but his nuances I always loved. The way he fixed his sunglasses on his face, with his thumb and his middle finger. The way he would laugh at a story by crossing his arms across his chest and leaning to the right and howling. The way he talked. The way he laughed. The way he walked. The way he would say certain words. The way he hugged. The way he shook hands. The way his eyeglasses perched on the bottom of his nose while he was looking over them. The way he left his keys, wallet and sunglasses in his upside down hat on the kitchen counter. The way he slept. The way he brushed his teeth and raised his right foot behind him. The way he drove. The way he scratched his nose. The way he'd sneeze once, look up directly in the sun and sneeze two or three more times. The way he'd eat pistachios. The way he loved. The way he never met a stranger. The way he would take his wallet out of his back pocket and open it up to pay for our coffee. The way he watched golf on TV. The way he played golf. The way he told stories. The way he told tall tales. The way he would exaggerate a story and wind all of his friends up into a tale that was only partially true. The way they would eat it up until they realized he was pulling their legs. The way he thought that was funny. The way he loved kids. Not just our kids, but all kids. The way all kids knew that about Mr. Neff. The way he always included a kid if we were going somewhere. The more the merrier. The way he'd laugh when some of the neighborhood kids would come to the door and ask me, "If my dad could play." Because he would – play that is. The way he got excited for all the kids successes and would just as easily go to one of the neighbor kid's games as one of his own. Just because he cared. The way he played wiffle ball. The way he loved wiffle ball. The way he could get a whole neighborhood to play wiffle ball. The way we all felt just be being around him. Wes made us all better and we all knew it. This was not exclusive to the kids and me, this was everyone that knew him. The way he made everyone feel special. The way I felt special being his wife.

Thirteen

I was home this evening and Sean called. He had just gotten off work a couple of hours after he was supposed to. He was upset. Work is usually the culprit or more likely what he can put his finger on. Grief is the real culprit, but that's hard to decipher. He came home around 8:30 and sat down with me to watch TV and talk. He said, "I cried today Mom. One of my technicians' father died this morning." We talked about it for a little while and then he went to his room and changed his clothes. I went upstairs to let the dogs out and when I came downstairs he was lying on the couch and had both of his hands over his face. I didn't catch on at first and at a sideways glance I said, "Oh no, what's wrong?" He was sobbing. It breaks my heart to see the kids suffer like this with the long, deep pain that we can't seem to get relief from. I held him and we both cried for a while. He is longing so much for his father. Every day is a struggle.

I slept okay last night, but when I started to wake, I felt all the tension come back. I went to bed with a headache and thought that sleep would help, but I woke up with it this morning. Clenching my teeth and holding myself rigid is horrible. I felt like I'd played a game of tackle football, alone of course, but nonetheless combative. I hurt. My body hurt. Watching Sean last night in the rawness of pain in grief seeped into my sleep and hurt me through the night. I woke up and wanted and needed Wes even more. It was Sunday morning again, and it was torture.

It's my birthday. The first since Wes has been gone. The day goes by pretty well. The kids are all home and they are insulating me. Jake is home from school, but will need to go back this afternoon. All four of us go to Costco and buy snackies for the Redskins game and all the necessities for a college boy and his apartment. We all watch the game and it is fun. We all miss Wes. We loved watching the games with him. But all of us together today was a special gift to me and I drank it up, all of it.

I am getting pressure from my counselor to take Lexipro. She is worried about my sinking into this deep hole. I'm worried too, but would like to climb out without medication. This journey through grief is the toughest battle to fight, for me personally. I'm not doing it well and it is beating me. It's beating me down and I know it. I agree to take the antidepressants reluctantly, because I know I am heading down a path I may not be strong enough to handle. The pain is too much and is overwhelming me on every level. I agree to take it but refuse to take the whole amount. So I cut them in half. I am surprised at the decent day I have. I'm surprised that I am having calmer days. I am so happy for the reprieve. I am relieved to get a break from the pain. And I think to myself, Really, is this it? Am I over my husband? Am I done grieving? It is surreal to the point I can't believe it. Then it hits me. I am on the medication, that's what is doing it. It's not me. It's not my ability to handle what is being thrown at me, it is the medication that is blocking my emotions. This medication simply cuts off the receptors in my brain and makes me feel like I am done grieving. If I wasn't in such a tough place, I would have stopped right then and there. But the fact that I was struggling so much and on a downward spiral unsure that I could stop, I made the decision to stay on it for a month or six weeks, still only taking half the dosage.

What I realized through this time was that I needed a break from the pain. That actually was a logical step. And needed. But I also recognized the fact that I had to allow myself to feel the grief, to step through every bit of it and to not suppress it. Situationally, sure it's okay to suppress, but not to ignore the reality of abject pain. I felt certain, that although I needed a break, I also needed to allow myself the time to regroup and gain strength, to go off the meds and to go for round two of the grief war. And so I did.

Dulling the pain is nothing new. People do it all the time

with alcohol and drugs, but this ran counter to all that I believed in and felt was truly the most beneficial way to handle my grief and the path it was laying out for me.

As conflicted as I was to actually go on Lexipro, I was equally conflicted about staying on it. What if I actually took the whole pill without cutting it in half? Would I act as if I was never married? It almost makes the grief feel fake or like I'm in someone else's body. This really bothered me to the core. It was a weird feeling to go from such intense raw, gut wrenching pain to almost feeling nothing, just calm.

Today is our twenty-eighth wedding anniversary. I start to reminisce about our rehearsal dinner and start to feel melancholy. I can't help but have this constant thought: How do you celebrate your wedding anniversary with only one person? I guess the answer is you don't. Another hurdle. Another first.

I am reading a book on grief that Wes' sister Marcia gave me. On some levels it helps to see the written word describing the pain, the longing and desire as well as anger towards God and doctors, for friends and family that are not going through this loss. It helps but it hurts. I think for me, all of Wes' friends feel the loss as much as I do and so I know that they are hurting immensely. Why does this realization help me, and is that bad? I guess I just need to know that I am not on an island absorbing all of the pain alone with no one that could possibly understand it. Yet they do, because they are on the island with me.

It's the first of October. We are already talking about plans on how to tackle our first Christmas without Wes. I let the kids decide. I give them the option of skiing like we usually do over the holidays or going someplace warm and sunny that will hopefully evoke some happiness. That's what we decide on. We do the opposite of what we normally did with Wes (skiing) and schedule a trip to the Dominican Republic with Nancy and Kevin and their kids. Once there, we will meet Laurie and her family that will be there as well...

I talked to my friend Bob today. He said that God has a plan. I told him I wasn't talking to God anymore. He said that I could tell him to say hi to Wes. I told him that I say hi to Wes all the time, I just talk directly to him and bypass God altogether. God didn't listen to us while we cried out prayers begging him to cure Wesley. He ignored us and ignored me. I don't believe in Him anymore. I struggle so much over the God issue and the fact that I've lost my faith along with my husband. These losses are huge for me, they are monumental. I simply can't reason out all the prayers begging for mercy and grace and just being left with feelings of abandonment. It's a rotten feeling.

So much has happened, and time continues to go by and I am just there for the ride. I don't even watch the scenery. It doesn't matter. I don't even see it these days.

We're in the holidays now. It is Thanksgiving. Our first without Wes. Our neighborhood sponsors a Turkey Trot 5K and this year it is dedicated to Wes. Wes' family is here and so are the Goons and our other neighbors and friends. We have a party after the race back at the house and the house is packed. It is so generous of everyone to be there and to join us. I am in awe of the fellowship as much as I am in a funk over the reason we are all here. Competing emotions always present, always conflicting. My goal is to start off the holiday with some long needed joy and laughter. The kids and I need it. In fact our whole circle needs it, and it really is a joyful day, no matter how deep the emotions run underneath. The party is great. There is a lot of food and drink. We have what Wes loved, and including Bloody Marys, mimosas, beer, wine, and coffee and Kahlua with Bailey's. That is a very smooth cup of coffee, so I have another. We decide to make it a tradition. It's hard to get bombed by 10:00 a.m. when you still have to cook a turkey, but all is well.

I was over at my dad's last night and he wrote notes on his steno pad, which is how he keeps his life straight. They are the controls he's put in place to combat the memory loss. He was always scheduled and methodical, but this is his way of keeping his life straight, as best he can under the circumstances. I read on his pad a note he wrote and it was obviously free thinking as he wrote about Mommy. It said, "I miss Colleen. Better for her to be in heaven with God than be here lonely and sad." I yelled inside, to myself, "Holy hell, what the heck?"

This note was so disturbing because my mother passed away thirty-two years before and he never remarried. I've watched him since Wes died and I cry all the time because my new reality is his reality and I'm not sure how to handle it, so I don't, I just cry. This note does nothing to help assuage my fears and my overall sad disposition. I am living my dad's life. He was stronger than me, that I'm certain of. But he never stopped loving my mom and he never stopped missing her. I know how you feel Daddy, because I'm feeling it too. Although he talks about Mommy a lot, I've never seen anything written even remotely like that. It has weighed on me heavily and I'm not sure where to put all of these new emotions. Does anyone not understand "UNCLE" anymore? I give up.

We are a week away from Christmas. Our first one without Wes. Another first. Another heartache. But I am determined to have joy in the house. It's funny what you can promote on the outside while you are still crumbling on the inside. I've gotten inordinately good at it.

We approach Christmas gingerly, but we go out the night before the night before Christmas and visit with friends. I go to bed and the kids come in raucously at 1:00 a.m. Jake comes up to my room to check in and he comes up to my bed to talk. I believe there was more in his system than beer. I'm pretty sure this was a liquor night, but nonetheless he wants to wake me up to talk about Wes. He was hugging me and I wasn't sure if he was going to cry but there was a knock at my door and I thought it was Kara and in walk Mack and Chris, two of Jake's best friends from our cul-de-sac. They were all born on this street. It was crazy. I couldn't quite get the info out of Jake about what was going on but Mack and Chris let me know that Jake and Sean and all their friends were out drinking and Jake and Sean were taking shots together. I'm a mother. I am proud. Proud of the flow of information leaving the lips of the drunk kids on the street. I learned more and more as the minutes went by. They tried to get Jake to help him to bed and there was a little fun resistance and Jake fell over. Of course he did. What else should I expect from 1:00 in the morning on the night before the night before Christmas? Like this happens all the time. The boys got Jake to his room at which point he had a burst of responsibility because his pup Mia was getting a little scared at all the loudness going on. As he opened the front door to let her out, Sean and his buddies came up the walkway. Good grief, doesn't anyone sleep around here? So I ended up with a gaggle of drunks in my foyer, with Jake mouthing off a little to Mack and Chris, but luckily for him they had their funny fuses on, and not their pissed off mode, otherwise Jake might have gotten smacked. Instead they took care of him and actually got a kick out of him. Funny, what people think is funny. I was straddling that line.

As Sean and his buddies walked up, Jake was taunting Sean and I was asking him a ton of questions. Sean was pretty inebriated as well, but he actually reminded me of Wes. He was staying calm even when Jake was pushing his buttons. My foyer was not big enough for six big drunk guys, so as Jake was joking and pushing Sean they start playing the game. For the record, drunks that play games with pushing and shoving rarely end up laughing. Being the sober one in the bunch meant I needed to separate this crew stat. All was fine, a lot of laughs and ribbing, but I couldn't help but think, *Wes, this is your job*. Yours to handle these boys of ours. These grown boys that are actually men.

We go to the Dominican Republic for our Christmas vacation. Christmas Eve was tough. I felt like I was in paradise and in hell all at the same time. But we did a lot, we had a great house and we had a lot of fun. There were a lot of laughs and I think it was worth it for us to do sunshine and get away from our normal holiday routine and change it up until we could figure out how to tiptoe back into our family traditions.

We stay through New Year's and with January in full swing, we are all heavy in the anticipation of Wes' one year anniversary. Crazy how in grief and with loss these firsts mark such a huge void. And yet we anticipate them with an unnerving dread. I still don't know if it is because we want to get the pain over or because it is our monument to our loved one, but whatever it is, it is daunting and punishing.

I am in such pain, as much as I was the night Wes died. How can I go on? I am crying gut-wrenching cries. Loud and primal again. I miss him so much it physically hurts. As we approach the one year anniversary I am turning upside-down and inside-out with grief. It's as if grief has grown another head. People think I should be moving on. After all, it's been a year. Like one year has a magic shut of valve and grief be gone. It doesn't work that way. But even if it did…

move on to what? Where do I go and what do I do? I know nothing different. Someone tell me what to do and where to go and maybe I'll do it, but otherwise, I've got nothing. Unfortunately, I can't move on because I'm overwrought with this grief, still. With this pain, still.

I have been regressing in the last three or four weeks. I can't believe it's been a full year. I don't even remember getting here. It only seems like two or three months. I can't believe I've gone a year without Wes. He was my rock. He was my life. I will never move past him, because I cannot.

I talk to someone who gives me a pseudo-outline on how to cope with the day to day, not just with grief, but professional life as well. So I start to make lists that I can adhere to. This is a new concept, to organize your grief. It feels like moving a plane on the tarmac at Dulles Airport.

I always think about how Wes made me feel or how I felt just by being around him. Peaceful is what comes to mind. Wes always made me calm. I just felt stronger and more at peace being around him. Contentment is the great equalizer. It enables you to deal with so much more in your life as in stresses and hardships and certainly your day to day. Contentment…I had that once.

Fourteen

Kara misses Wes so much. The two of them were two peas in a pod. They were so close, as she loved being his little girl and he loved that she was. No matter what they did or where they went they had a blast. Kara always enjoyed being with Wes no matter what her age. She always got his sense of humor and they would laugh about everything. They never had an argument. Even if something came up, Kara would never want to disappoint him and really there wasn't much she could have done to disappoint him. There was a bond between them that was as beautiful in its simplicity as it was in their shared adoration. What a gift she gave to herself to have gotten so much out of him for the time they had. She never wasted a minute or an opportunity to be with him. There was never any pressure from Wes – he wasn't like that.

They truly just enjoyed hanging out together. Blessings.

I take Kara to the airport so she can head to California and interview with Warner Bros. It's a big deal. The prospect of her leaving is daunting to me and I try to avoid the colossal upheaval this will bring in my world, but I know it isn't about me. I assure her that this is her life and that she needs to live it. "I give you my permission and I give you my blessing, Kara…go and live your life as you should." It is what Wes would have told her as well.

I realize that as my life unfolds, the difficulty is that there is always some kind of emotional overload that tries to prevent change and slow down progress. It keeps me from adjusting. I am struggling to just simply adjust. I realize through all of these major changes that each of my children has a significant other that helps them. For them those things remain constant. I realize that I don't have any of that anymore and recognize that as my life parallels my father's, I understand him better and better.

I start going to a Good Grief counseling group at the Life with Cancer house in Fairfax. We've had a break and we are back and I realize how much I have missed my grieving friends. They are the only ones that understand. I resisted going to group counseling. I reasoned that nobody lost a Wes Neff, but after my first session, I realize that everyone lost a Wes Neff. Everyone's loved one was as special as Wes. What I appreciated in the development of this group was that they had us all share our loved one with each other. So each of us got to know each other's spouse or child or sister or brother and it became personal. We had to bring in 3 things of our person's and share those things with the group and explain what they were and what their significance was to our loved one. I was moved by the love. I was touched by their devotion to helping someone they loved with cancer. I was thankful that my grief group was for people that had lost their loved ones to cancer. I realized quickly what the great benefit to all of us, was in sharing this similar bond of losing someone to cancer. First of all, we didn't have to explain the hardship of every lab test, every CT scan or PET scan, the devastation of chemo and radiation and the slow demise that those treatments alone have on the body and soul of the person you love. You just cannot explain the gripping fear and anxiety of every one of those tests. Every doctor's appointment and the anxiety of the news and the revelations about your reality. No one can really get it intimately unless you've walked those halls with your spouse or loved one. Cancer is a ruthless game. It's a mind game, it's an emotional game and a physical game, and it is so hard to watch it happening in front of your eyes with no way to slow it down, reason it away, make sense of it, and unfortunately for those that didn't win the battle, to sit by the bedside and watch it take the ones you love the most.

I come to realize that this group has something that I need. Something I need badly. And that is the shared fear and the shared loss and the shared experience of walking the cancer walk by the side of your loved one. We all need each other. I am thankful for this group and for Life with Cancer.

I am alone in a huge house, which irrespective of its actual size just grows by leaps and bounds exponentially, and every day I am in here by myself. It feels like a mansion and if I keep going like this I'll be living in a coliseum before long. My favorite place, my safest place and my happiest place, my home. Now it's becoming a symbol of all things lonely. How can that be?

I have dinner with Jane. She has been my beacon. I say to myself over and over on my darkest, hardest days, "But Jane is doing it and she's still taking steps." I look to her and it pushes and propels me to keep going. I know that both Jane and I have crawled a lot of those same miles over the first year. Crawling and gnawing our way through. Life isn't easy. She tells me she had to sell the things that were about Mike in order to move on. That included their houses. It was such a bold move and not one I can make yet. If ever. But those are things she accomplished in the first year after Mike died.

Our one year date is tomorrow, but it feels like it's today. I ran five miles with Kara today trying to distract myself and I worked until 9:00 p.m., then watched TV with her. I can't distract myself anymore. The one-year anniversary comes in and I relive every detail of the evening in my head. Memories can be heartless in these instances, but for some reason, I want every bit of it. For some reason this cataclysmic event in our lives brings me closer to him in some weird way. I have lived 365 days without Wes. It is hard to believe. I don't remember so much of this year. That is what shock is designed for. Keeping you in a bubble to insulate you from the pain. It's a necessity.

I remember right after Wes died, I couldn't even conceive of this day coming. I will never make it; I will never survive a year without him. How did I get here? Writhing on the floor in primal screams not thinking I could take one more step. I fear, that on this huge anniversary, I feel even more alone than I did before.

I wake up reliving it all again, like it was yesterday. The memories are that vivid. I can't really remember this whole year, but I wake up this morning and feel like the horrific event just happened.

It's February 3rd and I survived the day and the year. Laurie and Nancy plan a day for the kids and I. Jake is at school and he wanted to stay there. Kara and Sean took off work, as did Laurie and Nancy to stand by us and bring us into this next year but mostly to help us through the pain of this anniversary. We pick them up and we all drive into DC and go to the Newseum. It was a great day, but it was harsh in its reality. Again, opposing and competing emotions always at play in the world of grief. We went to lunch afterwards and I was in the shock bubble, but still conscious of all that Laurie and Nancy were doing for us, completely for us, but maybe for them too. They loved Wes as well. I could hardly wrap my head around their generosity of spirit walking this walk on this day with Kara, Sean, and I. My gratitude overflowed. I am blessed in the friendships of a lifetime that stop what they are doing to comfort a worn out, tired and beleaguered friend and her kids.

The kids tell me that it was a good day, and that it was a good idea to go to the Newseum. They said it was actually therapeutic because they realized looking at all the news clippings that their suffering is not the only suffering going on in the world and that some suffer so much worse. Really?? I am shocked that is their take away from the outing and I am more shocked and embarrassed that I am not the one teaching them this lesson, but indeed, it is they who are teaching me. They are right and shame on me for being so consumed by my own plight that I don't have the capacity to inherently understand this. I am truly consumed by my own situation.

This lesson sticks with me, as do the lessons of our best friends and their unselfish doting on all of us. I love them for it. I love them for organizing this day, even though I was reluctant to go. They forged ahead and made plans that I followed. I've been doing what they tell me to do for so long I hardly noticed, but I was ushered into a new year with them by my side. Thank you, my dear friends.

Later that night Wes' brother and sister in law and younger sister Emily come over and we order Chinese food. We told a lot of Wesley stories and laughed. Sean decided that Wes played golf yesterday on his anniversary and shot a 68. I love that story. I love that thought. I love that boy. Thank you Sean for giving me a positive image and a fun image to languish in. It gives me comfort.

We all meet at Dolce Veloce tonight to be together for Wes' year anniversary. All the Goons come and our neighbors and friends. It is an amazing evening and I can't help but feel Wes is there. I keep imagining that every time I go to greet a friend I can feel and hear Wes in my head say, "Hey, how you doing?" He was always glad to see people, and friends came from far away to say hi and to be there for us, but more so because they all loved Wes. He was just a special person and I bet he would never have guessed how many people he touched in his lifetime. Wes impacted people in more ways than he ever knew. I was actually just starting to realize the impact as well. He was just special.

I am taken aback again by the show of solidarity from our friends and family. The kids and I feel insulated and we feel grateful. We are blessed to have so many people in our lives that make us feel special because they loved Wes so much. It ends up being a great night, with so much love around, but sorrow too, and as I leave I am emotionally exhausted by the sheer weight of losing Wesley. I feel the loss from everyone there and I absorb it all, because I get it and I breathe it every day. I feel everyone's pain, because I share the same pain. We all are one in our loss.

I think people inherently believe that the one-year mark means a natural progression into something greater and a push forward. I beg to differ. In fact what I am learning quickly, that year two becomes harder, much harder. As I approach this next leap, I realize that the shock bubble is wearing off and I am no longer insulated by that and reality is coming through with fits and burst forcing me to deal with it. The fact is that Wes isn't here and somehow, I've got another year like last year and I don't have a clue how to get through it. Here we go again. Round two.

After a full year of grieving, I am as bad as I've ever been. I simply don't have the strength to keep fighting the hurt. I think that is what is so hard for me. I am so worn out trying to manage the pain and grief that I don't have the will for it anymore. I begin to understand what it means to die of a broken heart, I'm certain that is what is happening to me and I just don't care. As I move into year two, people expect me to move on, but I stay planted in the mud and can't move. Although we try, we don't go far. It's more like a shuffle. Shuffle here, shuffle there. I feel like I'm ninety in year two.

I come back from the beach and I feel guilty. I can't reconcile being there when Wes isn't. Guilt: my constant companion. Sean is at work and calls to check on me. I started to crumble on the phone so hung up. Sure as rain, Kara calls and says, "Hi Mom, what are you doing?" Code for, "Sean just called me and is worried." They have gotten especially adept at this Morse code of "checking on momma." I'm onto it, but even so, they persist. I don't fight them, because I have no energy. Try as I might though, I can't hold back and I start crying on the phone. I break down which makes Kara cry and it isn't fair to do that. I chastise myself for dragging them into these downsides, but often, I just let it rip, like now. I have tried to deal with this rough patch on my own, but it's too hard. This doesn't get easier for me, only more daunting. I'm worse off now than I was before. At least that's what it feels like, this minute, this day. Time will heal, that's what I'm told, but no amount of time will heal this ache. This ache is here to stay. I'm heading for the couch. Call me when this hell is over.

Kara followed up our call with several emails. Am I really supposed to get good advice from my child? Or maybe, who is the child now? I feel like I am. I'm not sure, but she's an adult and she had some poignant things to tell me.

She said, "Mom, we're not just around for the good things. Life isn't all good, but Dad made the best of things and he wants us to be happy. So we have to try to do that for him. He loved the beach and he loved that house, there is no need to feel guilty there. He wants you to enjoy it. That's the reason he built it."

I write her back, "Thanks for that Sweetie, heavy but true and good to hear. I love you."

"Sorry it's in an email, easier to write than say. But if things that made him happy, make us happy, then there is no reason to feel guilty."

"That's true. I got so much joy knowing how much he loved it and how comfortable he was there."

"Well, I hope you feel that way when you're there, knowing he is not physically there, but he's there. That always helps me."

"It helps me too."

I am comforted by the collaborative forces of my children and their concern for their mom. They are articulate enough and grounded enough to see a bigger picture, and their perspectives are probably better than mine at this point in time. I am thankful for them, always. Wes would be proud of them, as am I. Thank you, Kara for walking me through and giving me insight to which I could not summon. I love you.

Sean is flying out to Florida for a job interview with Smokey, one of Wes' closest friends and a fellow Goon. He has offered Sean a job and he thinks, as does Kara, that it might be time to bolt and start a new life and see what all is out there. I encourage him and we all take him to the airport. He is nervous for all the reasons he should be. It's a big move forward in his life, as it would be for Kara if she moves to California.

As life continues on right under my nose, while I try to stay cemented in the past, both Kara and Sean are moving. Kara to California and Sean to Florida. As I walk past their rooms and see them pack their belongings, I yearn for life as it was, but try to embrace the process of growing up. I try to assimilate all of these changes while trying to keep my wits about me. Wits that are nonexistent these days, but I am trying to act as if I have them, for my children's sake. I brace myself for the onslaught of emotions that will overtake me when they both are gone.

Kara leaves to go to her boyfriend's graduation, so I drive her Prius down a few days later to meet her in Savannah. Sean packs up his trailer and meets us in Savannah as well. As if this wasn't a mean enough joke, the two of them start their respective jobs on the same exact date. June 11th. I am amazed at their bravery to explore. I help Sean pack up his things, and try to shut down the voice in my head that tells me they will not be back. They will never live in this house again, under the same roof with me, and this realization cuts me like a knife.

We all meet up in Savannah, and have breakfast in a little café on the sidewalk. We sit down and I try to absorb it all. Kara will be saying goodbye to her boyfriend as he stays one more year to get his Master's degree. She and I will head west in her Prius as Sean heads South. It is the most surreal moment of my life. I say goodbye to Sean, Kara says goodbye to her boyfriend and Sean and Kara say goodbye to each other. We all hug and kiss and cry and I am left trying to figure out what the hell I've done in my life to deserve all this compounded pain. I'm yelling "uncle"…is anybody listening? Oh Christ, no one's listening.

As Kara and I head onto New Orleans, I am in a daze. I wasn't too great to start with, but now I am willingly absorbing more pain. I tell them over and over they have my permission and they have my blessing. I want them to go, and they need to go. Dad would tell you to go as well. I tell them, that I have to learn to make a life for myself and that I will get through. I will walk on. I don't totally believe it, of course I don't, but I make a good show of it, or at least I think I do.

We drive through the desolate span of Arizona. I am driving and she is napping. She has her music on because she may be more of a music freak than me, but thankfully we have similar taste. As I am driving in the solitude of the isolated road, Van Morrison comes on her playlist. "These are the Days" comes on and the tears start rolling down my face with no sobs, just utter sadness. Memories of Wes and I slow dancing to this song after he was diagnosed invade my head space and I am so sad. I can't make the tears stop and I don't even try. I cry for Wesley, I cry for the memory, I cry for the distress we both felt at his diagnosis and prognosis. The need to protect him again still hits me hard on this desolate road and as Kara opens her eyes and sees me she says, "Mom, what's wrong?" There are no real words to say to her or to explain the silent but prolific tears.

So I quietly tell her the song made me think of Dad and made me cry, and she turns it off as I struggle to regroup. We make great time out to California, we get there and get her moved in. We make the obligatory trip to Target, just like in college, and get her studio apartment set up. I feel that I am the daughter and Kara the parent on the road trip, because she took the lead on her move and I went along for the ride and moral support. Maybe in the end I wasn't the most help.

On Sunday, she takes me to the airport and I won't be getting in until 10:00 at night. I tear up on the plane as I know that I will have to take a cab from the airport because Wes will not be there to pick me up. Wes was never not there to pick me up. It was a condition in him. He would never dream of letting me take a cab, and for him, it was never an inconvenience. As I disembarked at Dulles and walked to baggage claim, the tears started and I could feel Wes sitting in the seat waiting for me with his shorts on, mint green golf shirt, and white baseball cap. I wanted more than anything to see him sitting there. I expected to see him sitting there and the reality of me hailing a cab to take me home, to a dark and empty house was literally almost more than I could handle. Welcome home to your new reality. You are officially alone.

I am back at the beach and we all meet up at Sedona's. Smokey is up from Florida and we, and the Goon crew all meet up for a drink. Smokey tells me that Sean came and knocked on his door at their office and asked if they could go out for a drink and talk. Smokey thought it had something to do with work and told him to come in and sit down. Sean asked him if he would tell him stories about Wes when he was in his twenties. Smokey said he and Sean started crying and laughing as they told stories about

Wes. As he relayed the story to me, he and I were both crying at the bar. It has meant more than I can adequately express, how all of the Goons have been there for all of us.

Sean told me that not long after this conversation between the two of them, Smokey suggested that he might benefit from talking with the Deacon at his church. So they both went over for Friday morning Mass and a meeting that had been arranged for Sean to go and speak with the Deacon. Sean called me afterwards and told me about the meeting and how much it helped him. The Deacon told him that God never said it would be easy, He just promised that He would be by your side. It helped Sean enormously, and helped me some. I was still angry at God, but forever and eternally grateful to Smokey for taking the son of his dear friend and mentoring him, not only in business, but through the pain of losing a father. My gratitude is beyond words.

I am getting my act together in some ways. The Seagull Century bike race comes around and I have Carol, Dale, Sherry and Ronnie at the beach. The race is at Salisbury University in Maryland. I get to the beach early to get the house ready and go to the grocery store. I am a little nervous about having guests, because I am the hostess alone. I'm not sure how to do that. But, in some respects the grief has me in a place where I cannot absorb anything more and so I can go through the motions without having anxiety. As we ride the sixty-five miles, it is a beautiful day. It was a lot of fun and I was constantly wondering if Wes would have made the trip with me and if he would have liked to ride in a race. I think he would have, because we always liked to ride the trails. These races are just ramped up a bit. So I was able to put a positive in my column because of the race and I was proud to have accomplished that. In the darkness, I have some light and I am thankful.

Fifteen

My dear friend Sandy has been my neighbor for over twenty years. She told me of this very real, very vivid dream she had had the other night, and said she spent the whole night with Wes. She said she woke up with a smile on her face and that they laughed throughout the whole dream. They were at the beach with the Goons and family. In the dream, he was sick, but looked as handsome as ever, but didn't look or act sick. She said they had a great time and she asked him if he was okay and if he was scared of the outcome. He said no, he was fine and that I was going to be fine too. He went through the list of things he had taken care of for the kids and me and that I would be fine and that Sandy needed to tell me that. I was quietly crying while she was telling me the dream and true to Sandy's nature, she was telling it as if it was an event she had just attended. It was funny in her retelling of it, surreal because it seemed so real and sad because I wanted to be in the dream with them. She kept telling me she spent the whole night with Wes and they had the best time. They always did, especially in real life.

I went to bed wanting to spend the evening with Wes as well. Sandy's dream affected me and Wes was on the periphery again and I was hoping he would show up in my dreams, but more so, I was hoping he'd just come home.

Thanksgiving comes around for the second time since Wes has been gone. Kara and Sean stay in their respective cities and it is just Jake and I. We get up and walk in the Turkey Trot with Greek, Barb and their girls and then we come home and get ready to hit the road for the beach. We have dinner with Jimmy and Sheila. There is a fire going and the Redskins game is on, a perfect combination for the day. I get up Friday morning and go to Wawa for coffee, still trying to relive my mornings with Wes. I go to the beach and it is flat, still, and calm. It is a cool morning and there are already many people out there enjoying the wondrous morning. I decide to start walking. I feel energized on the beach and I'd like to say at peace, but the truth is, I still cry most of the way as I talk to Wes and tell him how much I miss him. He loved the beach and this still beats me up as to why I get to be here and he does not. Will I ever reconcile this part of my heartache?

I am still struggling through the loss of Wes, and I simply

can't let go. I am still married to Wes, it's what I feel anyway, and it feels as though he is just on a really long Goon golfing trip. I wish you'd just come home already. But as I suffer through these years with the constant burden of trying to figure it all out, I rely on these dreams I have of Wes. I feel as if he prods me through the day to day by pushing me to move on and to start living again. I still don't want a new life, I still want our life, the one we had. This becomes the obstacle in moving forward. I still have one foot in the future with the other planted solidly in the past. Grief continues to keep me close. Close to Wes, that is, and I'll take it because it's where I want to be. He was always the steadiness and strength in my life and my example of the person I always wanted to be but I never had a clear understanding of what that was, until I realized that example was Wes. The purest, most genuine person I've ever known.

Coming into the second anniversary of Wes' passing with heaviness and dread. The kids are all gone, and I am trying to figure out how to get through this day in general, but also how to stay under the radar. It's so hard, and yet I anticipate that people may think it is time to move on. Okay, fine…but move on to what? The burden of that question weighs me down.

As I am struggling with this upcoming event, Kara calls me late and we chat for a long time. She keeps me on the phone, trying to help me adjust to this anniversary. When we hang up, I get a call from Sean, who tells me he is heading home from Dulles Airport. He was coming home to surprise me and be with me so I didn't have to do this anniversary alone. He says he'll be home in thirty minutes. We'll walk this anniversary together, he tells me. I hang up the phone and burst into tears. I couldn't believe how relieved I felt the second he said he was home. I felt that relief immediately: my son, my kids, my blessings.

I realize again and again that there is a need to feel this pain. I am conscious not to shut it out but rather to try and embrace it for what it is. It's real and its raw, that's what it is. But I also know that there have to be limits, if not timeframes set, at least some. Not in any concrete means, but set so that you at least attempt to move through the pain. What I fear so much is that I won't be able to move through the pain and it will always be there, and always be hard, daunting, and suffocating. The hope in the beginning of this grief journey was simply to get through the twenty-four hours that lay ahead of me. Now, I have transitioned into thinking I may never have the shoulders strong enough to carry this amount of pain for the rest of my life. My fear is that I will lose energy just to keep walking. This grief thing is so hard.

I sit in amazement of the outsiders that think the two-year mark makes it all better. It does not. But things have changed in the grief game for me, to be sure. I am doing better about being productive during the day and trying to find new things to focus on. But what may seem apparent on the outside is nothing close to what's going on in my heart and in my head. But yet, I keep walking. So people believe I am moving forward, and maybe they see something I don't, with clearer eyes and a clearer head, but my heart says it's not so. I hear people say that I'm strong and although I appreciate the confidence I almost look around the room to see who they are talking about. Surely, it's not me. Inside my heart and head I feel as weak and vulnerable as a kitten on almost any day still.

It's Life with Cancer's Lobsterfest time again. We are setting up for the event and I stop to talk with the director of Life with Cancer. My voice of reason through so much of this. I tell him how much it still beats me up that I couldn't find the right combination to get Wes well. I admitted that it cuts to the core of feeling that I just wasn't smart enough to figure it out. He tells me that you can't control cancer and that Wes' was a very complicated cancer, and that no matter what I did, it probably would not have saved him. He told me that I worked harder than anyone he's seen to try to save Wes, but what I gave him was all the love and support that he needed to know how much he was loved. This gut punches me, because it impacts me in a way that I need to hear. It is exactly what I need to hear. It assuages so much of my guilt as it also allows me some peace. Throughout all of the grief that I struggle with daily, I am equally stressed by my father's situation and taking care of him. The majority of his care is not on my shoulders but it is daunting in its sadness. I cannot wrap my head around the sadness in my heart over losing Wes and every day I am assaulted by the anticipatory grief of losing my dad. The question is not if, the question is when. All of my dad's issues weigh so heavily on me because it brings up so much sadness and stress and I still don't have a productive way to handle it, if ever. I white-knuckle my shifts with my dad, because I am constantly waiting and dreading the sorrow which is sure to follow. I cannot escape the sadness.

There is a very good chance that my grief cycle and experience has been hindered by my father's situation. I mean really, how do you move on from grief, when you have the next grief obligation breathing down your neck? In my case, I couldn't. I try to retreat, I try to stay under the radar, I try to steel myself to get through and not feel the pain, but it is there, ever-present, and ever weighty on my mind and on my shoulders. More pain to carry. Can't a girl catch a break? I realize that I am hanging on to my father for dear life because I simply can't handle the alternative. But my father is simply existing and that is not what the Colonel would have ever wanted. I know that because we've had this conversation a million times over the years. I realize that I have to let go and if it's Daddy's time, then I will have to endure. There are so many more tears over this realization, that I barely can grasp it all. But there it is. Grief and pain have resided not only in my head and heart, but surely all around me living and breathing. These combined grief experiences are overwhelming me to the point of desperation.

I am at the beach and I wake up early after having a totally convoluted, unhappy dream about Wes. In the dream we were breaking up because he found someone new. I could really use a break on these dreams – they are totally beating me up. But I get up and I get to the beach, because I am really distraught over this dream. That's the problem with these dreams about Wes, they are so emotionally charged that I wake up often being completely disheartened and sad. That was the case with this dream. The beach is hot as blazes at 8:30 in the morning but I take off running because I am feeling overwhelmed by the sadness and I am afraid I am going to have an anxiety attack. I figure I will try to run, or maybe and probably, try to outrun my anxiety. I couldn't stop the tears from rolling down my face and I also couldn't stop the gripping fear of the future. Isolation was hitting me hard at this point as well. I couldn't figure out where I fit in anymore, if I fit anywhere at all.

I order the book *Choose Yourself* by James Altucher. Not really a self-help book, but maybe a kick in the pants for some people, and that someone may be me, if the truth be told. I finally finish it after weeks of carrying it up and down stairs, from the beach to home and back again, but I complete it. It talks about resentment and anger and how they both essentially keep us living in the past. I'm living in the past. I am. It's my comfort zone. The past is my life I still want to be living. It's where I learned joy and had contentment. The future scares me. But his point is well taken as is the realization that I hold on to anger at God for not coming through for Wes. Am I supposed to have comfort in knowing that Wes suffered so much? It breaks my heart on a daily basis until it breaks my spirit, and that it has.

I get a call from my sister Patty to tell me Daddy is having a really bad day and that we think this is the end. I need to come over to Daddy's and Patty, Kiernan, and Meg and I all have to meet. I as the executor have to make some decisions. But first, she needs to tell me something: Kiernan has lung cancer. The words hang in the air and I don't even know what to say or where to go with all of this. Can this really be happening again? Now with my big brother, my only brother in a sea of crazy, dramatic girls. She tells me that Kiernan wouldn't let anyone tell me, in fact, wouldn't let anyone tell Daddy either. He didn't want to worry us, and so they kept it from me. But Patty said that since we would all be over there at Daddy's and I would see Kiernan with no hair, she didn't want me to be emotionally ambushed. Thank you Patty, for the forewarning. It was hard enough hearing it on the phone, but I would have been a disaster. He has been undergoing chemo for the last several months. They found a tumor the size of a golf ball, but couldn't do surgery because it was too close to his heart. The chemo has reduced the tumor to the size of a marble. Now they can do surgery. His surgery is scheduled for September 16th, my father's ninety-first birthday.

Kiernan knows how Wes' death has torn all of us apart. And now he is entrenched in it as well. He knows that cancer patients eventually get to the acceptance of death much sooner than their loved ones and it's the family and friends left behind that suffer so much.

I start sobbing on the phone for my Dad, who we think

we are losing more in the immediate and now for my brother, with whom we are not sure what the outcome will be. I am so guarded about my emotions these days and now I have no defense. I am vulnerable to all the pain of cancer and loss once again.

I steel myself on the ride over to my dad's as to how I will react when I see Kiernan. My 6'4" handsome brother would show the sure signs of being a cancer patient. He would be bloated from the chemo and have no hair. He would be wearing the ever-present baseball cap, every cancer patient's security blanket. I pull up to the curb and they are out in the garage and in the driveway. I see him and walk over to him and give him a hug and break down immediately. I only come up to his armpits so that is where my face is lodged. I am sobbing and he is holding me saying, "Sharon, it's going to be okay… stop that, you're going to make me cry as well." I detach myself from him and stand with him talking and he looks good, but said the chemo has been a "motherfucker," one of his favorite words from as long as I can remember. He tells me he won't do anymore. Chemo, that is. He's done four rounds and that's it. He can't do anymore and he won't. I'm trying to process all of this, all of his words and sentiments, and trying to assimilate them as they relate to my experience with Wes. I try to envision Wes saying he wouldn't do any more after four sessions, but I can't process that reality. Kiernan looks good, but he is now a cancer patient. I am smack in the middle of cancer again and I want to run, but I can't. This hurts too much, but

I can't leave. I don't want to think cancer anymore, but I must. I am in the armpit crying, after all.

As it turns out, on this particular day Daddy is not in fact dying, but has had a resurgence of Colonel power and is now coming around with the tweaking of meds and although moving slowly, he is up and about. This is the worst cycle of emotions imaginable. It never ends for me and on this Sunday, it has hit every corner and every extreme of emotions that I am not capable of curtailing or corralling. Put a fork in me, I'm just done.

But not so fast—we have to take my Dad to the doctor, instead of the emergency room, because he is living on this day and not dying. So Patty meets me there and as always seems to happen with the Colonel when he is at the doctors—he becomes the Colonel again at warp speed. The surely dying Colonel of yesterday becomes the standup comic again in the doctor's office. It is like a trip to outer space, I kid you not. He tells his doctor he was raised on a farm, and he is still doing it all. He's still mowing, taking care of his house and yard and you know, I was a B-17 bomber pilot at twenty-two. Oh my God. You would never have known that he was so ill the day before. You can't keep this cat down. The WWII heroes, they will not be kept down even when you are sure they are on their way out, they will always surprise you. My father always surprises me. That's just a fact.

We all show up at Georgetown Hospital for Kiernan's surgery. The other girls were able to see him and his wife before they were called back to prep. I got there and the nurses said we could go in and see him before they take him back. As the youngest of six, I am the last of the ducklings following into the surgical ward and I am stopped short by emotions. As I follow in my usual place of last, it didn't really register on my emotional Richter scale of what it would entail to see him before his surgery. I start getting choked up. I quietly grab Patty's arm and tell her I'm fine, but I think I'm going to stay out in the hall. I don't want to cry in front of Kiernan and the tears are just sitting behind my eyeballs ready to roll. I ask her not to make a big deal of it, but I was not going to go in. "Please just tell him I love him."

Patty said later it was the first thing he asked: "Where's Sharon?" Patty told him I was fine but was getting choked up. Kiernan was in surgery for ten hours. The news was all went well, but they definitely recommended he followed up with radiation. Nothing in his lymph nodes. Great news. I had to leave to let the dogs out. When the girls went up to see him, he asked, "Where's Sharon?" Man am I ever weak.

Patty and I went to see him on Saturday and he was high on morphine but his mental acuity was amazing. I would have been dumbed down on that stuff, but not Kiernan. He was citing facts and books and articles, it was unbelievable. Kiernan started telling stories about Wes and he started saying something about me being a schoolgirl. I didn't know where he was going with that story and I started to well up. A nurse came in and he was distracted, thank God, since I wanted off that subject as quickly as possible. But he picked right back up when the nurse left. Crap. But he said the first time he met Wes, he came right up to Kiernan with his hand out and introduced himself. Kiernan said it was so natural, and so easy for him that he thought, "Finally a sister I won't have to worry about. She will always be taken care of." How true. But now Kiernan worries about me. I know how you feel Kiernan, I worry about me also.

I had another dream about Wes and we were together, married and happy and the kids were younger. I remember hugging in close to Wes. He had his jeans and grey sweatshirt on and I was in there for a hug. It felt normal and safe as it always did being hugged by Wes and I tried to stay in slumber to keep the dream going. But as I started to wake up, I thought, Good God Wes, you are confusing the hell out of me in these dreams. He's either breaking up with me, divorcing me, having his old girlfriend in his dreams, or he's loving me like life used to be. I can't keep them straight, but I have suffered for those sad dreams, to be sure. I will take these dreams any time, any day, because they feel the way we used to be, the way I still want it to be. As I go through the motions of moving forward by trying to stay active and involved, my heart stays exactly in the same place. It stays with Wes. I can't budge it off of him, not even with a crowbar.

I watch the morning news show and they had John Kelley on, who is a psychic. He was so logical in his conversation, and said people that lose a loved one never lose the connection. That love and devotion is there forever. Their energy is around us always and they communicate to us in any form they can and sometimes it's through other people. I feel the connectivity to Wes all the time and his energy is fierce. I believe in all of that. Maybe it's a stretch, but I feel him around me all the time. I had another incredible dream about Wes. We were in our bed at the beach and he had his clothes and hat on. But we were close and kissing and I remember feeling that he was right there but he was trying to leave or I couldn't quite embrace him fully. I'm not sure if he was pulling away or if there was something preventing us from being completely engaged, but as I have now become an expert on dreams and their meaning, I know it is because he is gone. But the feelings in this dream were so real. The want was so real. The yearning was so real. The need was so real…to be a part of Wes, in his arms, touching his lips and in his life. It hurt but was wonderful at the same time. I just wanted to pull him closer, to be in his life again and he in mine. For him to be my life again. These dreams keep me connected to Wes. It's hard to let go when your dream world is so intense.

I make an appointment to take Bailey, our fourteen year-old Lab to be put down. I know I should have done it years earlier, but I couldn't stand the thought of losing one more thing in my life with Wes. I can always see Wes with his strong hands on either side of Bailey's head saying, "Are you any good?" Bailey was a crazy dog, of the Marley type, and Wes would shake his head just watching this dog do the things he did. But it is time. Sandy keeps telling me that I will know when it is time. I think I knew a long time ago, but did not want to face this. So I make the appointment and they tell me I have to bring him in for an evaluation. I tell them quite firmly, that I am not bringing him in for an evaluation, that if I actually get him there, that is what is happening. They agree and we set it up for the next day. Jake and I take him and Jake carries him into the office. They don't even make us stop at the counter, they just had us walk right back to the room. I feel terrible for doing this, but Wes was an adamant supporter of not keeping your dogs alive and in pain. It's a natural cycle and people keep their pets alive more often for themselves than for what's good for the pet. I certainly have with Bailey, even with Wes' words circling around in my head. So the time is here, and we sedate him and I ask the doctor if we are doing the right thing. She says it is time. He barely has any muscle left in his legs anymore. She says what makes it harder is that Labs are so expressive in their faces and their bodies go long before their minds, so it makes it hard to feel confident about making the decision. I don't want to shut this door and I don't want to make these changes. But I know I must. We say goodbye to Bailey with tears that aren't shed just for him, but for all the losses we deal with. It's a rough process, albeit necessary and graceful.

Kara and Sean struggle with this because they are far away, and all the doors that are closing forever to our past life with Wes make us bleed more pain. Mass texts start blowing up our phones as Kara and Sean help us and each other from afar. Wes always called Bailey "Red Bastard," because that was his coloring, and Sean texted, "Rest in peace Red Bastard." Kara sent a picture of Wes on the couch in the basement taking a nap with Bailey, who was at the opposite end of the couch. She texted, "All dads and dogs go to heaven." So true.

I found some papers that I had written on about Wes. They were about reading a devotional about losing parents. Even as an adult, the author felt like an orphan. Can widows feel like that too? I do. Even with children. I feel rudderless. It said, "Gone are the people that nurtured me and shaped my life." That was Wes. He shaped my life and so much of my thinking. He made me believe there was a better way to live: more peaceful, more trusting, more loving, and kinder. He lived a hopeful existence and I loved that about him.

It is three years today since Wes passed away. It also happens to be Super Bowl Sunday, with the Seahawks playing the Broncos. I'm not really vested in the game, but I can't help relive what we would be doing if Wes was here. It's more about the adrenaline of the whole Super Bowl spectacle that becomes paramount to this huge game. I know we would be in the basement with a million snackies watching it, either here or at someone else's house. I miss the excitement Wes would bring to these sporting events, whether they were football, basketball, golf, baseball, or hockey. He was fun to be around, and so I miss that and I miss him on this Super Bowl Sunday.

I just miss Wes. I miss everything about him. I miss you Wesley, I miss it all. I miss your person, your hands, your smile, your laugh, your beautiful face, your sparkling eyes, your voice, your words, your humor, your walk, your arms, your legs, your feet, your kindness, your outlook, your fun nature, your understanding, your optimism, your encouragement, your confidence, your intellect, your calm nature, your presence, your strength, your wisdom, your watch, your sunglasses, your wallet, your hat, your gloves, your shoes, your jeans, your sweaters, your golf clubs, your smell, your life, your love, your kisses, your help, your trust, your goals, your work ethic, your hot peppers, your baloney sandwiches, your bagels, your Jack Daniels, your Jose Cuervo, your margaritas, your Wheat Thins and peanut butter, your Wheat Thins and cream cheese, your cucumbers and vinegar, your 7,11 coffee,, your run, your golf swing, your Chex cereal, your whole milk, your salads. I miss everything about you. I miss every part of you Wesley.

My good friend Bill tells me he thinks he could live alone and be okay with it. I said, "Don't we all, until we have to." There's nothing noisier than loneliness.

I finished my widow book and it has me kind of in a sorrowful and pensive mood. I'm not really sure what the emotion is but I have to go over to Dad's to take care of him tonight and I start getting more emotional on the drive over. The impact of my father's widowhood for thirty-four years is starting to affect me. It actually always has but I have been in a fog and have not wanted to think about it or address it because it is my life now. But it has been creeping in, and in a more substantial way and I have no choice but to acknowledge it. The magnitude of my father's loss is equal to mine. My father lost my mom and she was his Wes. I haven't wanted to go there in my head, but there it is. I get it Daddy. I get all that you've been feeling for all these years. I don't know how you have done it. I'm sorry I didn't get it more profoundly before, and I'm sorry that I understand it so well now.

I finally wash Wes' clothes. I have put his clothes and mine together for these loads. A familiar sight that is no more. Tears on my face even after all these years. It will be the last time our clothes are comingled. Loss.

Jake is leaving for work. I am in the kitchen watching the news but writing in my journal. We chat about the day, getting bagels ready and juice, and then he says goodbye. I say, "Okay Sweet, have a great day." He tells me to do the same. Then he stops and says, "Come here Momma and give me a hug," and he opens his arms up wide. I don't want to cry in his arms, because I don't want to be the downer so I keep it light, but go in for the hug with gusto. I don't know if he senses something, or maybe everything, or maybe just thought I needed one, which I do. I didn't know how much until I got it. I have tears thinking about what a gift that was to me this morning. I am low, but trying to act normal, internalizing all these struggles I feel and Jake gives me a huge hug and I think to myself, I can make it through the day. Thank you God, and thank you Jake for a hug that means the world to me.

My face is all wet again. Tears of gratitude.

We get news that our dear friend's eighteen year-old daughter passed away this morning at 10:30 to cancer.

Sixteen

I'm heading to our friend's house in Haymarket. It's only thirty hours after they let everyone know that their beautiful, youngest daughter had just succumbed to cancer. She was just eighteen years old, only by a month, with early acceptance into William and Mary, but never got to see or experience the college life. They gave her an honorary degree and she did get to experience that. When she found out, she pumped her fist and said, "Yes!"

I head over to their house with Bob and Bill. We are all dear friends from high school. I love that they all still mean so much to me. We were all aware that Sophie would probably leave this world sometime soon. But who cares, who wants to be a prognosticator for anyone's death, especially your dear friend's daughter?

When Bob called to tell me Sophie had died, we cried on the phone, but I knew that I also wanted to talk to Bill. I hung up with Bob and immediately called Bill and we sobbed together on the phone. We didn't even need to talk, we just held on to the phone for dear life and cried together. No words, just sobs. We understood. We didn't need to explain. Although, what we did need was an explanation. An explanation from the God that I no longer talk to, except to tell him to f-off.

I've been suffering from the blame syndrome since Wes died three years ago. I just don't get it. Don't you get something from God, for being faithful? Don't you bank some good breaks when it's really needed in the God bank, for Christ's sake? I learned the answer is no. No you do not. You do not bank any hours for good faith, and love of God. I've bought in to that nonsense for my whole life and truly believed faith and prayer, and a lot of hard work would get Wesley better, but it did not. Not even a little bit.

So the three of us drive over to Steve's house, with a silent dread that is palpable. What will we say to them? How can we possibly console them? I'm a rookie at this and I've been on both sides of this coin. Neither side is enviable. I hate them both.

We get there and go inside and of course there is a lot of family, but not too much. Steve's parents are there, his older sister, Steve and Janice's oldest son and their other daughter. We come in and I am at a loss on every level.

I've been here, sort of, and I've done this, kind of. Steve is in the kitchen with his sister and the kids when we come in. We hug and we cry in each other's arms. I can hardly believe how surreal this is. How can this be real? How can beautiful Sophie be gone? I don't get it. Janice comes down the stairs and I am immediately taken aback by how tired and worn out she looks. It is like looking in a mirror, knowing that I had been in that same place a few years ago. We hug and cry, but Janice looks too exhausted to even cry. She lets us know that she is an atheist, but a joyful atheist. I'm still trying to wrap my head around that one, I don't even know what that means. But as the night progresses, so does the drinking. Bill collects wine and so brought a couple of great bottles of red over to them. I carried one in, because I had nothing to bring, so let them think the good wine was from me. Even in their current state, they knew the score.

Their home was built in the 1780s and Janice has done all the research. She takes me on a tour of the house and tells me the history. There felt something inherently wrong about the house tour, but I just went with whatever Janice wanted to do.

She takes me to the other side of the house and we sit down to talk. It is just the two of us for the time being. Janice tells me that there is no one to blame. She doesn't believe in God, so she doesn't blame him. She and Steve are incredibly bright. She graduated from Duke. Her sister is a renowned cell biologist in Germany, and Steve's sister is a doctor. All their brain power could not come up with a way to beat the cancer, or at least out run it for a while. One of the things that beats me up so bad is that on some level, no matter how hard I tried to find the right combination to beat the cancer beast, I couldn't figure it out. I couldn't figure out the combo. I've beat myself up for not being smart enough to pull it off. But neither could Steve and Janice and all the people they had to help them.

On some level that lets me off the hook, sort of. I can reason it out a little bit more, iron out some of the wrinkles in my heart and in my head that say I failed Wes, I failed the person I was supposed to protect. How could I let that happen? I just plain failed. But here I am in the family room of the people that could have figured it out and they couldn't beat it either. Strangely, I garner some peace from this. Is that wrong?

So as I sit with Janice and she talks, she tells me that she doesn't blame anyone, there is no one to blame, it's just biology. Some people's bodies are just prone to this and will not resist it. She knew that Sophie could face this. Sophie always had some health issues and Janice said that's why she never wanted to leave her. She just wanted to be there for her. Intuition? Possibly. So as Janice speaks so melodically and commonsensically to me, I am so taken aback by her words, and I consider the possibility right then and there: does God complicate grief? I don't have a great answer for that still, but I have thought of little else. Does God complicate grief? If you are going to blame someone, who is going to be? The doctors? Maybe. The individual? Sometimes. But mostly we blame God or are angry at Him for not heeding our prayers. Janice does not have to lose sleep over this. But I do, still.

Maybe I envy her for this little slice of being a joyful atheist.

Our conversation turns to me, and about me, and how I am doing. I say I'm doing okay, feeling stronger, except for this. But Janice asks me the inevitable question that is on so many people's minds, "Are you dating?" God help me here, but the subject was out of the bag. Janice has always been that person in my adult life whose words, although I may only see her a few times a year, always impact me with simple but jarring acuity.

She has impacted me again. I tell her I am not dating and am okay with it all. I am figuring this new life out and trying to figure out what my next step is.

But I tell her I think Wes was just my person in my life and I doubt there would ever be someone like him. She says to me in that same rhythmic tone, "You know Sharon when you have your first baby and you don't think you could ever love another baby like you love the first, but then you have the next one and you do love them. The first child is perfect, but the second one is perfect too, it's just a different perfect."

"It's just a different perfect." This has stayed with me all summer. It rings in my head like a bell reminding me that maybe, just maybe there is another perfect out there and that I should not shut myself off from the possibility.

Maybe there are two perfect Wes' in this world.

Thank you Janice, for letting me come over and comfort you and Steve and your family. Thank you Janice, for giving me some of the most profound advice I have ever gotten in regards to loss, and how to rethink the same old game that I had been hanging onto since Wes passed away. Thank you Janice, for giving me a lesson of a lifetime.

Seventeen

The Chinese philosopher Lao Tzu said, "The journey of a thousand miles begins with a single step." Don't I know it. How daunting this message is at the onset of the grief journey, and yet after all these years, its validity is resounding.

I've been a widow for a little over five years now. It's a long road, baby. There were times that I didn't think I could pick myself up off the floor, or get out of the closet as I writhed, wailed and sobbed in the days, weeks, months and now years since Wes passed. Grief, the great keeper of love, life, and memories. It's what we hold onto for dear life, as it becomes our only connection to the one we lost.

I have struggled to move on since Wes died, and at the

same time there has been an inherent need to stay in the same place. Staying static became the norm and a comfortable place for me to reside. It isn't easy to move on from loss for so many reasons, but mainly, because there just isn't any place else to go.

In the beginning, my reality was that life would never be as good as it was. Never as joyful, never as happy. Wes was my joy and I didn't want to face the days or future without him. Why would I? So often I felt like I was in a lifeboat in the middle of the ocean with no land in sight with no rudder. I had no direction, because there was no land; none that I could see anyway. Wes was always my rudder. Without him, I was just floating, going nowhere. What screamed to me louder than anything was once again the absence of hope.

In the beginning, thoughts of Wes would run through my head like a constant video loop, with no start and no stop. I was never not thinking of him. As I tried to relive every moment we had together and replay every part of our life over and over in my head, I knew I was just trying to will it real.

When I look back on the transitions I've made throughout the last five years, I think that some of the smartest choices I have made since Wes has died have been in simply saying, "yes." This seemingly simple response in the grief world is actually excruciatingly complicated and emotional. It was never easy. I always needed an escape route, knowing I could lose it at any time. Having a way out, if I felt I was on the precipice of an emotional collapse, was paramount. It took a lot of premeditated navigation on my part. I wrangled with accepting each invitation, but I think I have said yes to the majority of them. Well, maybe a lot of them, but it takes a lot of energy to just show up. Every event in our lives becomes an emotional obstacle course of navigating each decision and how it is going to impact us. It is like powering through every minutia of your day pushing a thousand pounds. And that is just to get us through the day, or even an hour. My constant internal dialogue was always, Just do it Sharon, just try. Just go for a walk. And so I did. I said yes.

Every step in the grief process is a transition. Even when we are standing still, we are transitioning. Our minds never stop during these tough and dark times and even as the light starts to shine in, it is always on overload and in a constant mode of assimilating emotions and experiences and what it all means for us. The sensory overload is monumental and unrelenting as we grasp to make sense of this new life and new changes that have been foisted on us. The moving on part, in my experience, has been prodded along by the power of yes.

The ability to look outside of our grief and navigate a path that is productive actually eludes us in the throes of grief. We are directionless, rudderless, and too exhausted and depleted to even care on some levels. Grief is a thief of time, of minds, of goals, of our treasures, our dreams, of love and of life, at least for the time being.

As I try to reconcile all of this pain and grief, I always think about the words the director of Life with Cancer said to me early on when he told me that I would start to move forward from grief when I get tired of feeling so badly. That conversation has impacted me and has been a profound lesson as well, even when the reality of it eluded me. And as I have tried to harness the comfort I had in my life with Wes, and more so since he has passed, it has proven to be a difficult acceptance.

I remember when I was at the beach a couple of years after Wes passed away. A bunch of the Goons went out deep sea fishing and they had to leave around 3:00 in the morning. Jimmy is the one who always arranges these outings. We usually head over to his and Sheila's house in the evening, after they get back with their tuna haul if there is actually anything caught for the day. But when the tuna is out there, they bring it back and Sheila cooks it up, and we have a great party. She and I were on the phone talking about what we would make and bring for dinner, as Jimmy came in through the front door. With an upbeat lilt in her voice, she said, "Oh, Jimmy's home!" It was almost as if she was saying it to herself, but she said it out loud and the part I heard was simple happiness, contentment, joy and gladness. He had been gone since 3:00 a.m. and she was so happy when he came in. She missed him. I knew it, because I heard it in her voice. I recognized it because I had that, I did that, and I felt that about Wes. I recognized it because it's what I loved. I recognized it, because it's what I've lost. I recognized it, because it's what I miss so much.

I read a quote from Anais Nin that had a profound impact on me. It said, "There came a time when the risk to remain tight in the bud was more painful than the risk it took to blossom." I read this and slowly realized that what I had been doing for so long was simply existing. Staying in one place, cocooned in the grief bubble because it became safer for me than trying to navigate a world out there without my most trusted person. I was vulnerable after all, and so I stayed protected, but at a cost. There is always a cost to staying in your comfort zone. For me, I was protected, but also staying mired in pain, anger, and sorrow. To let this dominate me all of the sudden seemed to suffocate me, and so I was challenged in sorts, to blossom. I had no idea what that meant for me or how to go about it but all the sudden it started to make sense to me. I was able to step outside of my very real, very isolating grief and realize that I was slowly killing myself. I needed to change.

This is no easy task, but what this did for me was open up possibilities that I was shutting out, and allow ideas for a new way of living and a new thought process. This became a huge revelation to me, and I was grateful, albeit scared.

But even so, the question became…blossom into what? Become what? I don't even know who I am anymore. I have been straddling two different worlds for so long now and not being very successful in either of them. My past life kept me grounded, but mired in sorrow, and my future life scared me. Snakes shed their skin, which is what every person dealing with loss must do at some point as well. Shedding that skin leaves you vulnerable, wide open to the outside, which is why we have this unyielding need to self-protect. But it's also at the point where the risks to remain tight in the bud become more painful and at some point even tragic. At these crossroads, the risk to blossom becomes less of a consequence and more of a relief. The ability to release this energy force for the good, rather than trying to contain the emotional currency as our shelter, opens up a realm of possibilities for each of us and lays the groundwork for growth, and in my little world of Sharon, I call that hope.

As I reach the five-year anniversary of Wes' passing, I find myself back in my grief counselor's office hitting an alarming low, even after all these years. This five-year mark is kicking me to the curb, or maybe I'm just tired of the longing. It's getting pretty heavy to carry.

As I struggle to figure out where I go from here, my counselor reassures me that I am not leaving Wes behind. That all that we had, and all that we were, is the legacy and the fuel that I am, and will be bringing into the future. But my future, not ours. A reality I still struggle to deal with. As well, I am also being suffocated by my anger at God, again and still, for not helping Wes. I cannot reconcile the pain he had to endure, both emotionally and physically. It haunts me and so I hold onto that anger as a shield as I declare my love and loyalty to Wes. The only problem is, I find I cannot sustain this anger any longer, no matter how hard I've tried. So as I sit on the grief couch with my counselor, I tell her how angry I am at God. I keep looking up to the ceiling every time I reference Him and she asks me point blank, "Why do you keep looking up at the ceiling when you talk about God?" I answer, "Well, that's where He lives, isn't it?" She responds, "But why aren't you mad at cancer?" I say vehemently, "I am, of course I am." She says, "Okay then, why can't cancer be way up there where you think God lives, and God has been sitting next to you the whole time?"

As tears started to fall once again without urging, I was left to contemplate this bombshell revelation now sitting in my lap. Now what am I supposed to do with all of this? Truly, I have been living behind this anger for so long I don't even know what a life without it and without Wes would look like. But this session with my shrink quite literally has changed my life. Relief comes to me, as do the tears, and as they flow, I am speechless. I look at her with wonder and joke later that I'm a little upset I didn't have the emotional wherewithal to make that connection by myself. But grief clouds your thinking, and that's just a fact. So I leave the office exhausted but maybe for the first time in so long, a healthy exhausted. I've just tamed the grief beast. Maybe I have just tamed it, or managed it, but I'll take it any way I can get it because I am finding peace with this new and weighty insight.

What I have learned through so much of my pain and grief that has really spanned almost seven years now, is that we all walk different paths. My path has been laced with so many external pressures and losses, so it has not been an easy walk for sure, but it never is. Trying to grasp losing my father right on the heels of losing Wes permeated all of my thinking. Living in anticipatory grief as I did while Wes was sick and then while my father was sick took a huge toll on me. I shouldered more than I thought I ever could, but I did, and that's saying something.

We came up to Wes' birthday and Father's Day in the same weekend again, and I was sad because it would have been his sixtieth. But it was filled with more happy memories than sadness and that was a welcome revelation. I had a crazy dream about Wes the night before his birthday and a much more sedate, happy one the actual night of his birthday. He came to visit again, and I will take those visits anytime I can get them, as they give me peace and possibly understanding.

I have learned so much from each excruciating step of this journey. And it hasn't been easy, none of it. But I am here and I am finding contentment that I thought was lost forever. I am trying to forge a new life for myself where it is not all about loss. I want to supplant all that gritty, abject grief with joy, and now I think I can, and I think I will.

I realize that I can move forward without Wes, even though I don't want to but know that I must. I still need him as much as ever, but now I can rely on myself, with a whole host of children, friends, and family to insulate me and prod me forward. But I don't take their efforts on my behalf for granted and I don't take the love for granted either. I am grateful.

I am proud of getting up and moving out of the closet on those dark, dark days. My worst days, in fact. But I've realized in those bad times there was still a sound perspective lurking in the background propelling me forward. And moving forward, often without direction has been a quiet victory for me. I've learned to look at those absolute dark times and give them the reverence they deserve, because they almost killed me, but they didn't. I've learned to appreciate the broken woman I've been and realize that I've been building myself back up for the last five years. That too, hasn't been easy.

I've learned that love is precious and maybe time is even more precious. Use it wisely and make it count. I've learned to relish the lessons Wes taught me in our life together. I've learned to love freely and trust uninhibited. A gift from Wes who never let me down. I've learned to trust by his devotion. I've learned that I have been graced by God's blessing by having Wes in my life, even when I thought his passing was my curse. I've learned to cherish the memories of our time together and those with our children.

I've learned to cherish moments more and take less for granted. I've realized we should all be working on our bucket lists. I've been reminded again and again that life is short, so make it worth something. Be engaged and be present. Again, make it count.

I've learned that there truly is a heaven, because that is where Wes is. I believe in angels, because I believe they come to us in any way possible to help us walk this path. I've learned we just have to pay attention to the signs and relish them when we get them. I've learned that my dreams of Wes, especially the great ones are the best parts of my day, week, and sometimes month. Even if it was just for an hour, it's my best day ever. I've learned that Wes is as funny as an angel as he was here on earth. His starring roles in my dreams have proven to be as impulsive and whacky as any Wes tall tale or story or mindset. I realize I love them just as much in a dream, as I do and I did in real life.

I've learned that in every broken woman there is a resiliency that lies beneath, just below the surface, even when we don't know it's there. I read a quote that says, "A woman's strength isn't just about how much she can handle before she breaks. It's also about how much she must handle after she's been broken." I've learned to take this to heart. I've learned I'm broken, but healing. I've learned to understand and respect the resiliency, because it's what's kept me afloat.

I've learned it's more courageous to let go of the pain that is keeping me static. I've learned it isn't more loyal to hold onto the pain to prove your love. I've learned it's okay to smile to hide the tears. I've also learned tears aren't so bad.

I've learned to live in the present and not the past.

Maybe that is still a work in progress, but I'm trying. I have learned to be grateful for the moment and to be mindful. When I slip and revert to aching for the past, I'm learning to supplant that with mindfulness. I've learned that this is a conscious decision.

And I think most of all, what I've learned from this long journey of pain, loss and compounded stresses, is that I can endure more than I ever thought I could. I think I'm proud of that because it shows there is emotional fortitude lurking in the places that I couldn't always see, touch or feel, but it is present. And I believe that through pain, we find strength. Unbridled strength that often times is unknown to us, but it is there. It lingers for the opportunity to reveal itself and when it is called upon, it carries us to places that we often didn't know existed within our own beings and opens us up to new avenues for emotional and spiritual growth and then ultimately, happiness.

Eighteen

It is hard to rewrite loss when you feel it's the end of the world. But the grief journey has now become my point of reference. The point in which I realize that I have taken my harshest reality and pushed through so much pain and heartache in an unknowing quest to get here.

I am trying to establish a new contentment. Different from before, but maybe one that I can live with and nurture. Where one day I can find an inner peace and a place of calm that I can reclaim as my own and for myself. This has become my personal journey and my personal but quiet objective.

This revelatory understanding brings with it an enlightenment that growth begins when we realize there is still life outside of grief. Maybe before, I was just trying to adjust to Wes' passing. Today I am slowly trying to accept it. I love Wes with all my heart and will love him forever. I guess in the end – that is what I would have wanted him to know. And maybe I did that. Throughout the long cancer journey, fighting to right the cancer, fighting to keep him alive and ultimately to keep him comfortable and at peace, maybe Wes truly knew. That is my hope and that is my comfort.

To Wes, I owe the beauty that is my life. That was the gift he gave to me.

About the Author

Sharon Neff earned her English degree from George Mason University. Her debut novel *Until It Wasn't*, is a narrative of her personal journey through her husband's illness and subsequent death. Her blog *Travails and Conquer*, is an emotional litany of the process of grief and loss, as well as strength and acceptance. She is the mother of three and resides in the suburbs outside of Washington, D.C.

About Life with Cancer

Life with Cancer, a program of the Inova Schar Cancer Institute, has become Northern Virginia's leading cancer education and support organization. We offer a variety of programs for patients, survivors, and their family members to help individuals cope with cancer, its treatments, and survivorship in the best possible way.

703-206-5433 (LIFE)

lifewithcancer@inova.org